ADVANCED PRAISE FOR
You Will Know the Truth
BY LESLIE T. THORNTON

"What a terrific, galloping read. The women characters are badass, the details precise—from the courtroom to the Situation Room. Can't wait to see the movie!"

GEORGE STEPHANOPOULOS, Former White House Communications Director and network television anchor

"This thriller moves with wonderful pace and surprise but not without plenty of thought-provoking and entertaining moments. A host of compelling characters come together in this story in unpredictable yet believable ways. Leslie Thornton has an ear for dialogue and she taps her unique life experiences to weave a gripping tale of intrigue that immerses the reader into some of the diciest spots in Washington, D.C.—from dark alleys to courthouses and the halls of The White House."

THURGOOD MARSHALL JR., Former Assistant to the President and White House Cabinet Secretary to President Clinton, Former Director of Legislative Affairs, and Former Deputy Counsel to Vice President Gore

"Leslie T. Thornton has cracked the code of the D.C. thriller—in a world where we live with constant distractions, she has a created a novel so rich and engaging with plots twists you will never see coming, that I could not put it down. I squealed when twists were revealed. I could not get to the next page fast enough. It is the perfect read."

ALYSSA MASTROMONACO, *New York Times* Best Selling author and co-host of Crooked Media's *Hysteria* podcast

"Leslie T. Thornton's gripping legal thriller takes you from the gritty criminal trial courts of Washington to the awe-inspiring Oval Office—with stops in between—and she does this as only a real Washingtonian could. With every turn of the page, the plot twists to reveal the crazy intersections between Washington's villains and its heroes. Washington has sometimes been called 'a small town', but, whatever you call it, Thornton owns it!"

JAMIE S. GORELICK, Former Deputy Attorney General of the United States, and Former General Counsel of the U.S. Department of Defense

"From 'Who done it?' to 'Who did it!'... *You Will Know the Truth* has more twists than a bag of licorice. In a shocking finale, your emotions will be overwhelmed as you weigh the ethical dilemma faced by our chosen leaders. What would *you* be willing to do ... for the greater good?"

HARRY RHOADS, JR., Co-founder, Washington Speakers Bureau

"The next great crime-thriller author has arrived! Leslie T. Thornton has crafted a gripping tale that will keep you spellbound reading her page-turning novel until you get to the climactic finish. *You Will Know the Truth* has a riveting plot with authentic Washington, D.C. references and captivating, distinctive characters. She is a true Washington insider, with a comprehensive knowledge of how the city operates—from its gritty streets, to its fabled courtrooms to the hallowed halls of the White House."

RONALD C. MACHEN JR., Former United States Attorney for the District of Columbia

"*You Will Know the Truth* is a clever, non-stop thriller that takes political intrigue to the next level. Leslie T. Thornton's artfully written debut novel delivers riveting plot twists as seen through the eyes of richly developed characters perilously navigating Washington's closely guarded secrets. What makes Thornton's work so compelling is that her saga is peppered with vivid, stunningly accurate 'inside baseball' accounts that show she really knows her stuff. Don't miss it."

LARRY COCKELL, Former Deputy Director of the United States Secret Service

"A nonstop thriller that takes you from the grittiness of a criminal courtroom to the political intrigue at the centers of power at the White House. Thornton uses her insights as a criminal defense lawyer and D.C. insider to craft a story of murder, secrets and lies that leave you guessing until the last page."

KIM TAYLOR-THOMPSON, former Director of the Public Defender Service for the District of Columbia, and Professor of Clinical Law Emerita, NYU School of Law

"Those who know Washington will recognize the places and wonder why they haven't met these people. Those who don't should be prepared to become involved in a world where you never know what's going to happen next and can't wait to find out. Everyone will believe the story is one of Washington's deep secrets revealed by an insider breaking the code of silence…and who knows? If you like crime and politics, read Leslie T. Thornton's first book. You won't forget it and you'll be ready for her next offering."

ALAN WHEAT, Former Congressman

"Leslie T. Thornton has written an exciting, gripping and insightful page-turner that grabs the reader's heart and gut. This writer knows Washington, D.C. After spending much of her career living and working in this power-centered city, she learned a lot. She writes for the lifelong Washingtonian and for the rest of the world who live outside the Potomac. Whether you've spent much time in the city or not, Thornton's book teaches you all you need to know about the back-stabbing politics, the policies made for the few, and the everyday wheeling and dealing that so quickly becomes part of formerly normal men and women's culture. Thornton writes of a city that is for the powerful and not for the faint of heart. Not only is her book an emotional roller coaster, it is one you will want to share with others. Great writing. Great storytelling, from page one to the very end."

BOB J. NASH, Former Assistant
to the President & Director of Presidential Personnel

YOU WILL KNOW THE TRUTH

YOU WILL KNOW THE TRUTH

A THRILLER

Leslie T. Thornton

Published in the United States by Sweet Read Publishing.

You Will Know the Truth. Text copyright © 2021 by Leslie T. Thornton. All rights reserved. No part of this book may be used or reproduced in any manner whatsoever without written permission except in the case of brief quotations embodied in critical articles and reviews. Printed in the United States of America. For information, contact Theodore and Ann Burgh at Sweet Read Publishing for more information, sweetreadpublishing@gmail.com, 910-409-1076, 4617 Pineview Drive, Wilmington, NC 28413.

www.sweetreadpublishing.com

The Library of Congress Cataloging-in-Publication data is available upon request.
ISBN 978-0-986-09415-6 (hardcover)
ISBN 978-0-986-09416-3 (ebook)
First Sweet Read Publishing Edition: 2021.

Subjects: FIC031030—FICTION / Thrillers / Legal, FIC031060—FICTION / Thrillers / Political, FIC050000—FICTION / Crime.

Cover concept by Samantha Carlin
Cover design by adam b. bohannon and Leyla Erkan.
Interior design by adam b. bohannon.

Bible verses included are from the New International Version.
In limited part, inspired by real events.

FOR MY REMARKABLE FAMILY

Daddy—you called me and Libby your "pride and joy." We were only 20 when God took you away, so I have missed you for a lifetime. But I truly believe that some of the best parts of me were the best parts of you.

Mom—you were stunning, smart, a total badass—ask anyone—you would have stood in front of a train for your family, and often did. You always told me and Lib that we could be anything, do anything, long before it was the popular thing for mothers to instill in their daughters. Thank you for raising the girl that became this woman. For all the times you stood in front of a train for us. For reading the earliest draft of my novel and, unknowingly, leaving me with the most exquisite memories of your loving, embarrassed, scared, and funny expressions.

Libby—my twin sister, my other half, my giggle-buddy, my other heart.

Weaver and Hugh—my older brothers and giant supporters. Hugh, you wondered if we needed a family intervention after reading a particularly gritty part, and Weave, you wanted to play 'Rolex' in the movie, LOL.

YOU WILL KNOW THE TRUTH

CHAPTER ONE

It started off typically enough, at least for a case carrying the weight of overwhelming horror and abject savagery. Prosecutors skillfully outlined the sacrifices poor Mrs. Campbell had made trying to give her kids a better life than she had lived. They talked about how treasured she was in the community, the online fundraiser that was launched when her husband died, about why she was reluctant to accept the money. Prosecutors explained why she wanted to stay in a neighborhood even as it changed, became less safe, and took her husband.

It was hard to argue with. There would be no cross-examining the witnesses to Mrs. Campbell's goodness and grace. You sully the sinner, Nicki knew. You don't drag the sufferer. Especially not this one.

The prosecution had witness after witness lay out the painful story. The good and decent Mrs. Campbell, in her haste to get home from her second job in time to say goodnight to anyone who might be still up, cut through the back alley adjacent to her home on F Street, S.E. It was longer than she preferred—that alley—and darker. But she had taken that short cut a thousand nights before, and sometimes she'd made it home in time to kiss her grandson goodnight and say their prayers—a special delight because this grandson bore her husband's name.

That night, Mrs. Campbell heard footsteps behind her. They would not have frightened her though—lots of people in the neighborhood used that short-cut, almost all of whom she knew personally. Teenage boys mostly, racing home to make curfew. Among other innocents. "Don't tell Mom!" they would call to her as they tore by.

That night though, the voices Mrs. Campbell heard—the last ones she would ever hear—were not from people in the neighborhood. They were not teenage boys racing home. They were not innocent. They were lawless, felonious men who took her life with appalling disregard. What was the point?

CHAPTER TWO

"The law is a horrible business."
—CLARENCE SEWARD DARROW

Mrs. Campbell's murder left an appalling crime scene, even for one committed in a back alley already covered in the filth and stain of a ruinous neighborhood. A first responder threw up, the rumor went, and Nicki Jo Lewis, no surprise, pulled one of the case's four defendants. It was a terrible case at the center, it seemed, of ruthless and unrelenting gang activity producing some of the worst criminal conduct the city had ever seen.

It helped that Nicki's client was only incidentally connected to Mrs. Campbell's killing. Mrs. Campbell's wedding ring was "found in her possession." That's what the radio run said, but it was just police speak. Nicki's client was *wearing* it, showing it off—that's how police investigators found out about her.

She could have found that ring anywhere, Nicki would probably argue at trial—on the street, in that alley. Anything was possible in that part of town. Still it was a bloody mess; arguably the most monstrous crime to happen in Washington, D.C. since 1950 when some New York City gangsters got chased south and ended up with their tongues pulled out through slits in their throats. On Pennsylvania Avenue. Right in front of the White House.

"Officer, would you please describe what you saw when you arrived at the scene that night?" the prosecutor had asked a few weeks after Mrs. Campbell's murder at the preliminary hearing.

"The decedent, Mrs. Campbell, 55, was lying in the alley, on her side. Her dress was up around her waist and, and..."

"Please continue, officer."

Though a seasoned investigator, the officer had barely slept since he'd begun working the case. He could not get the images, the memory of poor Mrs. Campbell, out of his head. A widow, Mrs. Campbell had worked two jobs—both menial, so that she could help send her children *and* grandchildren to decent schools. People knew her in the neighborhood as someone who always smiled, no matter her own troubles, and always offered to help someone else, no matter her own needs. When her own husband was killed by a stray bullet just two years before, the neighborhood crowdfunded thousands of dollars so she could move herself—their children and grandchildren—to a safer neighborhood. But she refused to go.

"This is my home," she'd said. "It's the kids' home, with the only memories they'll have of their father." It was hard to argue against her reasoning.

"There was a lot of blood. A lot. A pipe was... protruding from her, from her..."

"From her what, officer?"

"From her, her... anus."

After two men raped Mrs. Campbell, a third shoved a steel pole so far up her rectum that it punctured her lower and upper intestines, her liver, and her pancreas, and scraped the bottom of her right lung. It was gratuitous. She bled out, but not before the contents of her intestines had poured into her stomach cavity and begun to poison her.

News reports had spared some, but not enough, of the particulars. Reporters had dramatically described Mrs. Campbell as a grandmother of thirteen (though that was hardly news in that part of town) who died a slow, agonizing death at the hands of street thugs. Thugs who hadn't just killed her, but who taunted and humiliated her before God took her home.

The medical examiner said Mrs. Campbell probably was alive through much of it. Widely reputed for his exacting work by the time he 'met' Mrs. Campbell, the ME said he had never seen so much internal organ damage in a human being who had not been crushed by heavy machinery. At the hearing, the ME tried to keep the description as clinical as possible, but the crime was so violent that even complicated medical terms couldn't temper its blow, and when he finished his testimony, people all over the courtroom were crying. One of the judge's law clerks got sick.

It was not great for the defense.

The ignoble misery, and Stephen King-like gruesomeness of Mrs. Campbell's murder, bothered Nicki. It was objectively shocking. But Nicki was one of the best trial lawyers at the agency—full stop—and the agency, by law, did not turn down a case for its complexity, or even general ickiness.

Tall and slender, Nicki wore her hair close-cropped, almost clean-shaven—sort of an anti-afro—long before the style was popular. It suited her. It was no fuss, much like her personality, except for the cluster of silver bangles she donned on both wrists that clanged when she walked and sang when she talked with her hands. Some days, the days when she was not in court, they went halfway up her arms. She wore jeans to work, but like all the other public defenders, Nicki kept a suit in the office for court.

Still, Nicki wore her jeans with a plain white t-shirt and a short, black leather jacket, winter or summer. She was opinionated and strong—gave you the impression there was nothing she couldn't do—and that was probably right. Nicki had high cheek bones, a warm smile which matched the charm that could take people by surprise, and good legs. Really good legs. She was whip smart, comfortable in her own dark brown skin, and she cursed. A lot. All the defenders cursed. It was part of being in the club, and a by-product of the ugly, violent world in which they operated. Nicki said "fuck," a lot, in everyday language and as expression, and she was the one they'd made a wager about it at the office.

Nicki's colleagues bet she would accidentally say "fuck" in court one day, be held in contempt, and ordered to pay a fine, and one day she almost did.

"Ladies and Gentlemen of the jury," Nicki had begun in her closing argument that day. "The government's only eyewitness told you a pretty tall tale today. Here is why you shouldn't believe it. Here is why you can't believe it. The government's only witness, the one witness the government has that puts my client anywhere near the scene, well, he was fu... I mean he was fouled up on drugs."

The judge had lowered her head—she was smiling—but some of the jurors laughed out loud. It was pretty funny, everybody said, and though she hadn't actually said the word, Nicki's colleagues made her pay up anyway.

Here, in this case, Nicki figured if all the government had on her client was the ring, her client would not be lumped in with all the other defendants whose fingerprints and DNA were on the pipe. Still—Nicki knew—you never really know, especially in street crime cases. Defendants tend to leave things out when they are telling their lawyers what happened.

"No more surprises," Nicki had told her client as they were preparing for the preliminary hearing. "If you lie to me again, I'm out."

"You can't do that," Miss Gray protested. "The judge will make you stay my lawyer. You're just a damn Fifth Streeter anyway."

Miss Gray, the only woman among the four defendants in the case, was wrong about that. Nicki worked at the D.C. Public Defender Service, PDS, and it was nationally known for the quality of its lawyers and the significance of its cases. By statute, PDS was assigned the most heinous cases in the system. By reputation, Nicki was known as one of the best trial lawyers in the agency—full stop.

"Don't bet on it," Nicki said getting up from the table. "Let's go, Shep." Shep was Nicki's investigator. He was already on his feet. He knew the drill.

"Okay, okay, *OK*," Miss Gray had said. "Tony's my man, you feel me?"

"Tony Allen?"

Miss Gray nodded.

"Tony Allen? You're telling me two days before preliminary hearing that you got that ring from one of the other defendants?"

Nicki was furious. She knocked on the door of the holding cell and stepped out with Shep.

"If Mrs. Campbell got that ring from one of the other defendants, well, that's more plausible than her finding it on the street or happening across it at a pawn shop."

Shep nodded.

"But it makes the connection to the killing closer than I want her, and it sure as shit won't help my motion to try her separately from these other heathens."

"I know."

"Fuck."

"I know. You were counting on a severance motion. Even without the ring, being tried with the other defendants will prejudice the case against Miss Gray."

"It's such a high burden under normal circumstances—prosecutors love to lump them in all together, and it helps the judge clear her docket faster," Nicki said. "Fuck."

Severance motions are notoriously hard to win under the best of circumstances, and Nicki hadn't won hers. So, late in an unusually cold winter, in the nation's capital, Nicki Jo Lewis began trial in a case the city had not seen the likes of in almost five decades. There was no way for Nicki to know the trial would only be the beginning.

CHAPTER THREE

The case started typically enough, at least for one like this, and proceeded, over the next couple of weeks with, alternatively, procedural tedium and unrestrained emotionalism. All the defendants' lawyers, including Nicki, were up and down from their seats with objections and "for the records," and little of it stuck. Periodically, Nicki sent Shep out to run something down, verify a thing, but as a general matter, the case proceeded apace for her client. No big surprises, good or bad. And, given the barbaric circumstances of Mrs. Campbell's death, that suited Nicki just fine.

At the end of the third week, still in the prosecutor's case, Nicki continued her trial routine. After court, she said goodbye to Shep, talked a little about the next day, and snuck out of a side door of the courthouse to avoid the press pool staged in front.

"Thanks!" Nicki waved to the court security officer.

"One of these days, they're going to figure out this side door actually opens from both sides," he laughed.

"You might be giving them too much credit."

Nicki hustled down concrete stairs to a one-way street adjacent to the courthouse where she sometimes found a parking space.

"You don't mean that!" the court security guard called after her.

"Naaah," she dragged out the vowel sarcastically. "I'm okay with the press. Mostly."

Early in her career, a younger Nicki believed that battling with the press was part of her job defending the downtrodden, the oppressed and—in her less experienced mind then—the misunderstood. A couple of armed robberies and gruesome murders "matured her thinking," Nicki once shared with a local crime reporter over drinks, as she learned the benefits of a mutual "trust but verify" relationship with the press.

Nicki hopped into her blue-gray late-model Audi, tossed her purse, briefcase, and other briefcase on the passenger-side seat, secured them from flinging all over with the seatbelt, buckled her own, cranked the radio and, bopping her head to Stevie Wonder's "Superstition," headed the five or six miles through the city, up Rock Creek Park, to the two-story-with-attic single family home on a quaint and quiet street known for its well-kept lawns and generational ownership. She didn't notice United States Secret Service Special Agent David Stackhouse (smiling, watching her bop her head) follow her up the parkway and slip into a parking space a couple of doors down from her driveway. She didn't notice him when he adjusted his rearview mirror to make sure no one had followed her. She didn't notice him when he checked both side views, made a call, slowly pulled out, and then headed back downtown.

Inside her house, Nicki poured a glass of wine and left it on the kitchen counter to breathe, jumped in the shower, changed into sweats, and parked cross-legged in front of the living room TV to catch the evening news and start reviewing her examinations for the next day. She just missed ABC *World News Tonight* but caught the tail end of a local news report describing "unprecedented law enforcement activity" around a row house on U Street, N.W.

That is some wild-looking shit, Nicki thought. *Waaaay too many police, fire trucks, helicopters, and undercover vehicles . . .*

Moments later she was cradling her phone. "Shep, Shep . . . you seeing this?"

"Yup. That's some wild shit."

"That's what I just said!" Nicki laughed.

"Yeah well, I've already got some calls in. Let you know if I find out anything. Working on your examinations?"

"Yeah."

"Then what are you doing watching TV?"

"Bite me."

"That's my girl," Shep laughed. "Don't stay up too late."

"I won't. But let me know, okay?"

"Yup. 'Night."

"'Night."

Ray Shepherd had been Nicki's investigator for five years, but he'd already had plenty of exposure to the seedy side of the law business. He was older and more experienced than many of the other investigators as well as Nicki, but they clicked from the beginning and had been together ever since. Still, there was something about Shep that Nicki never got. Most of the time he was warm, funny, witty. But sometimes during a case, out of the blue, he turned tense and burdened. At first Nicki thought it must have been the whole Middle East thing—the physical and psychological wounds left on a soldier from a war. Shep had a long scar down one side of his neck that traveled halfway to his Adam's apple. But there was something else. He drank hard. Not that that was unusual at PDS. They all did. It was impossible sometimes to get the taste and smell of the seamy side of the lives they touched out of their clothes, their hair, their minds. A good whiskey could do that.

But the way Shep drank hard was different. He was not like the other guys—drinking and swearing about the prosecutors and police, judges, and witnesses, re-telling their best trial victories, lamenting the disappointments—though he did that too. Rather, his was the kind of hard drinking you saw in a 50-something year-old man sitting alone at a bar, staring down at his drink, swirling the ice around with a little red straw even when there isn't anything left to sip.

For a time, Nicki blamed Shep's girlfriend. "The Girlfriend," Nicki called her, though not to Shep, never understood the dedication that PDSers had, not that most people did. The Girlfriend particularly did not understand the late nights. Nicki did not like that The Girlfriend was always accusing Shep of doing something he wasn't, and sometimes he'd come to the office in the morning exhausted from being up half the night arguing with her. Nicki knew the truth—all the defenders did. There was no better time than nighttime to try to track down the witnesses, shore up your case, find your client who didn't show up for court that day.

Anyway, Nicki thought Shep's girlfriend was a complaining, nagging, stuck-up bitch. She was surprised when he moved in with her anyway and, on moving day, he was so drunk he just swayed in the threshold of their new home, going neither in nor out. That was the other Shep, and it had long worried Nicki. But Shep's competencies were longer than his contradictions, and they worked well together. They had similar sensibilities.

It really wasn't any of her concern what was happening on U Street or Shep's, but they were both curious and sometimes the agency would be assigned defendants after that much law enforcement activity. She shook it off and put her head back down into the ugly case she had in front of her.

CHAPTER FOUR

"It is a man's own mind, not his enemy or foe, that lures him to evil ways."
—SIDDHARTHA BUDDHA

"This one's pretty bad," Police Captain Fisk said, walking toward his lieutenant.

"Why are you telling me?" Lieutenant Jackson said. "I'm not a rook."

"I'm just saying, it's bad."

The lieutenant thought his boss must have been having a bad night.

It's a stupid thing to say to a lieutenant in homicide, Jackson thought. *I mean, we've seen everything, pretty much. Brutal slayings. Decapitated babies who have been raped and sodomized before and after they were already dead. We even see the stupid piddly shit that's mostly disgusting because of who it involves. Like that time we found Congressman Bayler's body naked and beaten half-unconscious by that prostitute on 13th Street who got a little too excited with his please-beat-me-shit. How we managed to keep that one out of the papers is beyond me and for the life of me I still don't know why we took such pains to. It wasn't like he was an important congressman. Just one of the hundreds trying to find a way to make themselves important to someone other than lobbyists. What the hell was the Captain's problem?*

"Shit! Jesus Christ." Lieutenant Jackson had stepped inside the door.

The Captain was wrong. It wasn't pretty bad. It was unspeakable.

"Jeeezus Christ! What the hell is all this? Shit!" Lieutenant Jackson was rounding the hallway into the first room.

"It's gotta be a set-up," Jackson said, joining his Captain. "There's too much blood. It's gotta be fake. Or maybe it's a decoy. And the sick bastard is off killing someone else while we stand here with our dicks hanging out?

"How is that better?"

The U Street house looked like a horror movie set.

"Where are the bodies?" Cecilia said joining the two officers in an upstairs hallway.

Fisk and Jackson looked at her, then at each other.

"Brilliant, CC. We were just standing here ourselves scratching our butts, wondering what's wrong with this picture," Lieutenant Jackson said.

"Knowing you, you were scratching your balls. It was rhetorical, idiot. Or is that too big a word for you?"

Most of the guys in the homicide division liked Cecilia. When the male officers first started calling some of the other female officers "butch," Cecilia joked with them about it until she earned her place as one of the guys. Later, after they had accepted her (to her satisfaction), she gave them a bad time about it, and they took it. They stopped calling the other woman officers "butch" publicly *and* privately. It had always been easier for Cecilia to fit in, though. After all, her job didn't threaten theirs. She was strictly "crime scene," and she was good at it. They even called her "C" at first because it was cooler than Cecilia and everyone had a nickname. Then, when it got around how good she was, they added the other "C" for crime scene, and she ended up as "CC." It was fine with her. Her family called her "CeeCee" too, though for different reasons.

Captain Fisk and Lieutenant Jackson laughed with CC, but the tension was so strong it was already seeping into their muscles making them tight.

"Doesn't look like we can get very far into these rooms without disturbing the evidence," CC said.

"Yeah, the booties aren't helping either. We're sliding in them, and all that dark red against the brightness of the light blue—well, it just makes it all look worse," Fisk said.

"Not that that's possible," Jackson said.

"Holy Mother of God!"

Captain Fisk had left Jackson and CC and made his way across the upstairs hallway to another bedroom, tiptoeing in those stupid shoe covers. By the time Jackson and CC caught up with him, Fisk was just standing there, head lowered. CC thought he was crying.

"Oh . . . my . . . God." CC's voice was barely audible.

Captain Fisk was almost yelling. "Who or what in hell is capable of something like that?"

"Whoever it is, they're not done," CC said. "Or at least this isn't all they've done."

"What do you mean?" Jackson and Fisk said, almost at the same time, their heads spinning around in CC's direction like synchronized swimmers.

Jackson and Fisk had not worked together all that long by D.C. homicide standards, and sometimes Fisk got his back up if he thought Jackson wasn't giving him his due, like earlier. But they were good colleagues. They had been trained in the same old-school way of looking at things, and though many years apart, they had the same sensibilities about what being a good cop was: what it took, what they were willing to give.

"I don't think these bodies, well . . . these body parts . . . go with this blood," CC said. "Remember that year when that movie came out about the scientist who had gone mad and started killing people by eating parts of their bodies while they were still alive, and everybody was relieved that the storyline was not based on a real crime?"

"Yeah," Captain Fisk said.

"And police departments, psychologists, and even journalists searched their files for any links to something similar that had actually happened in the past or was happening in the present, just in case. People even researched archives in Europe and Africa and in some tiny little nations in

South America where the occurrence of cannibalism was rumored to be high. But there was nothing, remember? No one on the planet, it looked like, had committed in real life the depravity of deeds that were acted out on the screen, remember?"

"Yeah, yeah."

"Until now," CC said.

A long night of processing dragged into the early morning and it was still going on when D.C. Police Chief James C. Coley called a meeting of all the precinct's supervisors and managers; "anyone in charge" he had directed his assistant. A big man with a big reputation, Coley waited as his assistant counted every single person in the "call" room, and when she was done, he began.

"I'm going to say this one time. The U Street case does not exist to you. Do you understand that? If you are not directly working it, it doesn't exist. If anyone asks you about it, you don't know anything about it. You do not know who is working it. You do not know who has been to the crime scene. You do not know who's processing it. You don't know shit, understand?"

No one in the precinct had ever seen their boss in the state he was in. He had not once asked any of them to flat-out lie about an on-going investigation. Misdirect the press sometimes, sure. But not out-and-out lie.

"Chief, with all due respect, that's just not possible. I mean we've already started talking to possible witnesses, suspects, you know the drill. It's just not poss—"

"Make it possible, Captain. In fact, that's your job from now on."

Fisk, just back from U Street as CC and her team worked on crime scene processing, was well aware Chief Coley only used an officer's rank when he was in a formal setting or making a point. This day, Fisk knew, his boss was making a point not to be missed.

"And if I hear you have talked about this case to anyone without my permission, goddammit, you're out. Gone. I don't care if you're one day from your pension. I don't care if you're one day from your pension, your wife is pregnant, your teenage daughter just ran away, and your dog just died. You're out, goddammit!"

Captain Fisk lowered his eyes and turned his gaze toward his Lieutenant who was looking at the floor. Fisk could hear the wall clock ticking it was so quiet in the room, but Coley was hollering anyway. Then, just like that, Coley turned on his heels, left the room, walked the long hall to his office, closed his door, pulled the blinds on the windows, and called the head of the President's Secret Service detail.

"David? It's Coley."

"What's up, Chief?"

"Something's come up."

"Yeah, figured. You only call me when something's come up," Special Agent Stackhouse joked.

"Can we meet?" Coley asked.

"Of course."

"See you in fifteen."

The Chief grabbed his coat and hat, pulled his office door closed behind him, cut across the building by perpendicular hallways, and went out the back of the precinct.

Special Agent David Stackhouse had established the protocols for the two of them. Years ago, they first started working together pursuant to an inter-agency effort designed to avoid the 9/11 intelligence failures (failures attributed to a lack of law enforcement and intelligence agency cooperation) Since then, Stackhouse had found Coley to be one of the smartest men in his field, and a straight shooter. They had known each other for years prior and, after 9/11, they had worked more closely together ever since. Even when other federal agencies tried to push local law enforcement around, Stackhouse could always rely on Coley's skills and discretion. He had established the protocols to protect them both from real and political bad actors.

"You know every time I see you; I forget you look like something out of central casting," Coley laughed as he approached his colleague. "Don't you think this every-third-time-we-meet-change-of-location-shit is probably overboard at this point?"

"What, you gettin' too old to remember the sites?" Stackhouse laughed, drawing Coley into a man-hug. It was fifteen minutes on the dot.

"The United States Secret Service," Coley smiled. "Y'all live in a different world than the rest of us, to be sure," he laughed, shaking his head. "You still training with the CAT team every year?"

"Yup. It's good for the boys in the counter assault team to see me certify every year with them—it's good for morale," Stackhouse said as they started to walk along towards the Tidal Basin.

Tall, handsome, with broad shoulders and strong facial features, Stackhouse did look a little like something out of central casting. And he could take a man out with three fingers, maybe one if he got it just right.

"U Street, right?" Stackhouse asked.

"You already know about it!?" Coley stopped short to face his friend. "How do you know about it already, Stack? I mean, I have had it locked all the way down, and it's just a local homicide scene, anyway. I mean, what do you guys know, or care about it?"

"Jim. You know it's not a typical D.C. homicide scene."

"Yes, but that doesn't answer why a federal agency charged with protecting the president and his family already know or care about a local crime like this." They continued walking.

"Not that far from the White House, right?"

"Lots of crime happens not that far from the White House. You gotta give me something here."

"Does it matter? I mean, how do you see it playing out if we know about it?"

"It's just such a horror show; I'm trying to contain leaks in my own department, at least until we get a handle on what it even is. I don't want to worry about—"

"Jim."

"I'm not saying you guys would leak anything—I mean nothing gets out from you guys that you don't want out. I know that. You know I am not saying that. It's just the worst thing I've ever seen and-and if it got out before we have a handle on it, the panic, hysteria it could cause..."

They had long passed their usual turnaround point. Stackhouse was giving Coley the time and space he needed to let off some steam. The Service had kept so many of D.C. Homicide's secrets over the years, many Coley didn't know about. Stackhouse knew Coley was not really worried about a leak from the USSS. His own department, sure. D.C. Homicide leaked like a church roof, at times. Coley probably wasn't even all that concerned about how the Service found out about U Street; he had gotten used to Stackhouse's seemingly unending capacity for finding out the truth.

Stackhouse ducked under some low-hanging cherry tree branches, holding them back and away so Coley could get through.

"Coley," Agent Stackhouse finally said, "we were there."

"What?"

Coley's baritone voice echoed on the rushing wind and hung a bit. Stackhouse looked around to see if anyone were near enough to hear Coley's voice, then nodded left for Coley to follow him further away from the closest walkway.

"We were there—before you guys. On a tip."

"Why didn't you call it in to us, or at least to me?"

"Like you said, we didn't know what we were walking into, what we were going to find. Only that it was not going to be a typical D.C. Homicide case. If we were wrong, we would have turned it over right away. We weren't wrong. As you know."

"David." Coley was done mucking around. "David, how am I supposed to be thinking about all this? Are we going to have a fight over jurisdiction?"

Stackhouse did not expect the police chief to be happy, and he wasn't.

"We have a similar interest, Jim. This needs a lid."

USSS Special Agent David Stackhouse and D.C. Police Chief Jim Coley started the walk back along the Tidal Basin in silence, each man with his own thoughts, each man with own burdens, each man with his own responsibilities and, each man with his own principal—Coley's being the Mayor, Stackhouse's, the President of the United States.

No man can serve two masters, Stackhouse heard his mind telling him, reminding him.

"All right let's talk about it," Coley finally said. "It's really early but we think Sheila's niece may be one of the victims. I guess you guys think so too or you wouldn't have been there."

It had been an accident. Sheila was much too sophisticated in the ways of Washington to have made such a stupid mistake, but she had. When she found out she was pregnant she worried less about keeping it a secret for the sake of the President than about her own political ambitions. She was a player in presidential politics; Cooper had been a kick-ass-lawyer-turned-top-Democratic-strategist and kingmaker. She liked that people thought of her that way—big people, important people—teeing them up, or teeing them out. She had worked hard to get where she was and did not want that diminished by harsh criticism she believed would come to her with an "illegitimate child." But getting rid of it wasn't something she even deigned to think about. So, before she started to show, she took an extended sabbatical, told everybody she had inked a book deal, actually wrote a book while she was away having the baby, got the book published and saw it become a bestseller.

Later, Sheila began taking full-time care of a "niece" whose pretend-real-mother was too young for parenthood. A very small number of the President's Secret Service detail knew the girl as Abby, her real name, and she was officially, though secretly, a "protectee." And only two members of the D.C. police knew who "Sheila's niece" referred to—Sheila Cooper's daughter, and illegitimate child of the President of the United States.

Agent Stackhouse weighed his options. He trusted Coley—no question. But there was no way to protect his principal—the President—and also tell his colleague, and friend, the truth. But not telling Coley the truth meant Coley's investigative team would be spinning their wheels, wasting precious time and resources, all while dealing with psychological blows of such a jolting crime scene.

Still, a little deflection was needed here. Stackhouse reached into his breast pocket for his phone, entered his security code and took a few seconds to look at the screen.

"I've gotta go, Jim," Stackhouse said returning his phone to his pants pocket.

He looked directly at Coley. "I'm sorry. POTUS is looking for me. They're sending a car."

As he watched Stackhouse walk away, Coley knew not to call out after him. But he didn't get it. In CC's preliminary crime scene work, they had turned up some of Abby's clothing, a locket she had not once taken off since her father gave it to her on her third birthday and, possibly, a part of a finger. Sure, Coley thought as he made his own way back to his office.

It could have all been planted there to make it look like she was a victim, Coley thought.

But why hadn't Stackhouse answered him directly? Did he really get a call that the President was looking for him?

As Coley reached the location on the Mall where Marine One sometimes lands when there is an event on the South Lawn, Coley was stopped in his tracks by a new idea.

Maybe it was *Abby,* he thought. *Maybe the President did it, and the Secret Service is covering it up to make it look like a crazy person did it.*

Certainly, there had been years of rumors of the Secret Service doing all kinds of things to protect the indiscretions of a President. Of course, this wouldn't be covering up an indiscretion, it would be covering up a crime—a murder. Of a child. But there had been credible rumors of that sort of thing, even going back decades.

As he neared the Mall, Coley smiled at himself. His thoughts were getting the best of him. Still, there was that curious accident that killed all those agents in the 1960s that nobody ever explained. Later that night, after a long day of pushy reporters, unanswered and unanswerable questions, Coley shot up in bed.

If the Secret Service was there, Coley thought, his mind clear despite his fatigue and the lull of his bed, *it had to have been before the police got there because they sure as hell weren't there when the police arrived. And if they were there, why wasn't there the slightest hint of disturbance of the crime scene? Not one single footprint in all that blood. Maybe the President didn't do it at all. Maybe the Secret Service did it. On its own.*

That night was uneasy for Agent Stackhouse too. His top deputy, Lew Cornwell, one of the few people Stackhouse had trusted with information about Abby and other things related to the President, had called on a secure line.

"Saw Coley today. He asked about Abby. I'm sure he thinks either the President killed her, or we did."

"How do you know?"

"I know him. You know, we've known each other since when he was in the police academy in D.C. and I was in St. Louis. He is trying to figure out why the U Street crime scene didn't appear disturbed; he's remembering all those old stories about us. He is remembering that whole unit that was killed in the '60s."

"Do we need to manage him?" the deputy asked. "Or is it just as well so he'll back off? If he thinks the President's daughter is involved, he will leave things to us, and that would sure make things easier."

"I don't know. Cuts both ways," Stackhouse said.

"Who *did* do it?"

"Who did what?" Stackhouse said.

"Come on, David. We know they found some of Abby's things. What was the point of that whole *Mission Impossible* dangling-from-wires-shit we did over there last night if....?"

"Enough."

The deputy's mood fell a little. He could not remember the last time his boss talked to him that way, and David sensed it.

"Sorry. It's late. It's been a long couple of days. Get some rest and we'll talk in the morning."

"All right. The morning, then."

Chief Coley was settling back into rest. He had decided that Agent Stackhouse must have had a good reason and the conspiracy theories he had been nursing since they'd left each other on the Mall earlier were not worthy of him or his friend. Plus, didn't the involvement of the Secret Service, albeit secretly, get him off the hook a little? Maybe they would take over the investigation. It had only been a day and a number of the officers who were working U Street already were already showing signs of post-traumatic stress disorder. A couple of the crime scene personnel had already made appointments with the police counselor—something he would usually have to fight them to do—and one was already talking about retiring early. CC was working overtime to stay as scientific about the case as she could but the images from the house felt burned in her psyche and when she closed her eyes, she saw the crime scene as if it had been etched on the inside of her eyelids. Coley knew he was going to have as much to handle taking care of his own officers as he was with the investigation itself. The idea of someone else being in charge was starting to have appeal.

CHAPTER FIVE

"Mornin' Shep," Nicki said getting out of her car the next day. "Not even going to ask you how you knew I was parking here."

"You know you might think about changing your routine now and then."

"Yeah. I don't know. At least I'm consistent."

"So was Mrs. Campbell."

"Not sure if that was a cheap shot or not, but *touché*."

"Just looking out."

"I know. So? What's up? Find out anything about U Street?"

"Not yet. We got bigger problems."

Shep went around the front of the car to the passenger side and grabbed a bunch of Nicki's bags.

"What do you mean?" Nicki said from across the roof of the car. "You know how little I like surprises, Shep."

"His name is Rolex. For stupid, obvious reasons. Apparently, he wears Rolex watches—gold ones, platinum ones, diamond ones. There is a lot of trash talk around the way about whether they're real or fake; one day he challenged some guys to take one of them to a jeweler and ask for a certificate of authenticity."

Nicki tried to interrupt Shep, but he kept on.

"'Go 'head, man. Take it. Tell 'em you got that Rolex from a cat named Rolex,' he apparently said. 'Ain't nobody gonna' believe you.'"

"Nobody did of course," Shep continued, "and nobody seems to know really, about the watches, or the man."

"Shep! *What* are you talking about?" Nicki all but yelled at her investigator.

"I'm just trying to give you a picture of who he is," Shep said. "He is not on anyone's witness list. Not the prosecutor's, not on any of the defendants'. No one seems to know where he originally came from either, but he has an accent that sounds southern, sometimes; at other times less so. He wears lizard and ostrich boots almost all the time, even in the summer, but he has told people cowboy hats are 'punk-ass.'

"But at other times, this cat apparently speaks in such a refined manner—too refined even to know people in that neighborhood, much less associate with them—but he's been hanging around the F Street corridor every day until late at night for months. No one seems to know where he goes at night either. He just leaves a place, they say, and the next day he's back. Nobody sees him coming or going and a couple of guys argued over whether he even owns a car. Some of them swear they saw him getting on the bus, but others say they saw him driving a Benz."

"Shhhep," Nicki said drawing out his name. "You have ten seconds to tell me what the fuck you're talking about."

Nicki and Shep were almost at the courthouse. Much of the press was gone but for a few local radio stations and papers.

"Probably on the U Street thing," Shep said under his breath, nodding at the small gaggle of press.

"So?" Nicki said. "Ten seconds."

"So, this cat Rolex, he was there. He was at the crime scene. He was at the scene when poor Mrs. Campbell was murdered. He was in the alley. Standing in the shadows, or some shit."

"Are you kidding me? Don't fuck with me in the middle of trial," Nicki hissed. Shep, leaning in closer, just looked at her. "Who is he? What does he say?"

"No one can find him."

"No one can find him?! Do the police know about him yet?"

"Supposedly, they learned about him a couple of days ago and are out looking for him. I don't know if I buy that, though."

"So, we don't know who he is, what he would say about what he saw that night, whether he'll cooperate with the government, whether he'd cooperate with the defense—nothing, right? That's what you're telling me? For all we know, this 'Rolex' character could get on the stand and say that our client was there that night, right there, cheering those perverts on?"

"Or?"

"Or what?"

"He could say he knows our client wasn't there because he's the one who took the ring," Shep said.

"And gave it to her? Why the hell would he say that?" Nicki said. "Why would anyone believe some idiot named Rolex anyway?

"Unless . . ."

"Unless she was doin' him too," Nicki and Shep said at the same time. It was a preposterous theory, to be sure. That their client would be sleeping with one of the defendants, *and* the main witness, was preposterous. But they worked in a preposterous world, and nothing surprised either of them. Almost ever.

"Okay," Nicki sighed, threw her head back and rolled her eyes—a crappy attitude she needed to shed before she walked through the courthouse doors.

The inside of the courtroom was more crowded than they expected given the U Street news. Nicki looked around to see if there were any new faces—anyone on the victim's family's side, or the defendants', or where the press had squeezed together shoulder to shoulder. She nodded at the prosecutor's table, making brief but pleasant eye contact, and then direct eye contact with each juror. She made sure the jury saw her being fearless and agreeable. Because in a minute, she was going to tear the prosecution a new one.

Shep surveyed the courtroom as well, greeting the marshals, bailiffs, and the judge's chambers' staff. For a minute, he thought he saw someone he knew in the back, to the right, but when he looked again, Agent Stackhouse was looking down, obscured now by the two people sitting directly in front of him. Shep made a mental note, though.

The bailiff recalled the case—the same way he had done every court day for weeks now —while the judge flipped through the case file, then greeted the jury.

"Is counsel ready to continue?" the judge asked.

"Approach?" Nicki said.

"Is that a question, counsel?"

"Sorry, Your Honor. May counsels approach the bench?"

Shep smiled. He had seen Nicki get that way more than once—so comfortable in front of a judge that she sometimes forgot to observe all the formalities.

"Approach, counsel," Judge Sullivan said, and the whole gang of lawyers crowded around the bench—Nicki, the prosecutor and his number two, the lawyers for all the other defendants, and the court reporter holding her stenograph in her hand.

"Your Honor, we have just learned some important information that has a direct impact on my client's defense," Nicki began. "*All* our clients. We believe the prosecutor has known about it for at least a day. Maybe more," Nicki said.

Nicki had known Danny Holden for years. She had been on the other side of the aisle from him in countless cases. He was one of the top Assistant U.S. Attorneys in the District and he won. A lot.

"Ms. Lewis, this better be close to what you're implying, or you can forget it," Judge Sullivan said. "And counsel," the judge aimed at the prosecutor, "you better hope it's not."

Nicki was taking a calculated risk. If it turned out that the "Rolex" issue was just a big bust for her client, she would have interrupted the trial, accused the prosecutor of bad faith, worse—withholding evidence—and, if "Rolex" inculpated her client, jeopardized her own defense.

"Your Honor," the prosecutor began, "we did learn that there might be a witness who has certain information. But we have no way of knowing if what that information might be, and what that information really is, is the same. So, yes, we *have* been looking for a 'Mr. Rolex,' but we really don't have anything to report at this time."

Judge Sullivan grimaced. "AUSA Holden," she said, "would you like me to tell you what I think of that answer? And, counsels, is his name really Mr. Rolex?"

"He's known on the street as Rolex, Your Honor," Nicki said. "He wears—"

"Rolex watches, yes, I figured that, counsel."

"No one seems to know if that's his real name," Nicki said. She glanced back at Shep for any additional information, but none was forthcoming.

"Mr. Holden, if you do not present this witness by the end of this day, I will entertain a motion from Ms. Lewis to dismiss her client's case," the judge said.

"Your Honor, if I could explain further, I am certain you would—"

"Step back, counsel," Judge Sullivan said, banging her gavel.

"Your Hon—"

"You can step back, counsel, and we can continue with this case or I can have the Marshal step you back—you choose."

Nicki exchanged a glance with Holden. As a defender, it was a badge of honor to be stepped back by the U.S. Marshal assigned to the courtroom for vigorously arguing with the judge in defense of your client. Most prosecutors did not find the same honor in being taken to the jail behind the courtroom, and Holden wasn't an exception. All the lawyers hurried back to counsel table and sat down; Holden included.

"Call the next witness for the government," the judge said.

The next couple of hours dragged along, the defendants' lawyers taking turns cross-examining the last of the chain of custody and other technical witnesses. It would not be long before they wrapped their case, Nicki thought, and the defendants would begin putting on their respective defenses.

Lumped together as they were, there were not a lot of options. Nicki's goal was to try to distance her client from the rest of the defendants without throwing them under the bus; but she would, absolutely, if she had to.

The court broke for lunch before the government wrapped up its case. If they were lucky, the government would not finish before the day was over, giving the defendants another half day to start theirs. Nicki grabbed the little she needed for such a short break and headed for her car. Shep had left after the judge ordered the appearance of Mr. Rolex to continue looking for him. During an earlier ten-minute break when one of the jurors had requested to use the facilities, Shep and Nicki agreed on the strategy.

"I've got a line on the witness. Do you want to inform Holden, or do you want me to find this Rolex cat? If I can?"

Nicki paused, whirling the strategies in her head. "No real upside to offering a maybe, far as I can see. Holden owes me one. Judge gives me credit for fair play. Not a good enough return, especially if he puts my client in the alley."

Shep watched Nicki's body language as she weighed the pros and cons, waited for her to finish, satisfied she was getting comfortable with her decision.

"See you after lunch," Nicki said. "Be careful."

"I'm always careful," Shep said, squeezed her arm and headed to the side door.

Special Agent Stackhouse watched as Nicki blew into her hands and rubbed them together. The downside of the uninterrupted time Nicki got having her lunch in her car during trial: the time it took for the car to warm up on cold days. She kept her coat on and grabbed a protein bar from a bag of them she kept on the floor. She just needed a little in her stomach to get through the afternoon, particularly as it looked like the day was going to conclude with the remaining technical witnesses for the government. She read through her notes from the day, flipped through her cross examinations to check for anything she might have missed. The hour ticked by without incident; no one really noticed her hideaway parking spot behind the courthouse, except Agent Stackhouse, and nothing caught her attention. Halfway through the hour, Stackhouse made a call, started his car, and pulled out into traffic headed back uptown.

Nicki's phone rang and startled her. She looked around as if the ring were a car horn or a knock on the window before picking it up. Shep.

"Got him." Nicki held her breath. "I think he's going to be all right."

"Good. See you in a minute."

Nicki took the last bite of her protein bar and dabbed her mouth with a napkin. She gathered her files, checked around her for anything she might have missed, exited the car, and headed toward the courthouse. She went right in the front door, through security, and up the escalator. She wanted to see what Mr. Rolex looked like before she informed the judge the defense had found him.

"Your Honor, before the jury comes in, I have something."

Shep had beaten Nicki back in and was sitting on a bench outside of the courtroom talking with the man she assumed was Rolex.

"The defense has found Mr. Rolex."

AUSA Holden shot a nasty look at his own investigators sitting behind him, and then at Nicki.

"Counsel approach the bench," the judge said. She made eye contact with the prosecutor but addressed Nicki.

"Ms. Lewis, first, that's his real name?"

"Yes, ma'am. Apparently. I have not actually talked to him—my investigator found him."

"Is he here?" The judge looked around the courtroom, though she did not know what she was looking for.

"Yes, Your Honor, he's outside with Mr. Shepherd."

"Bailiff, please bring Mr. Rolex to the bench," the judge said. After a moment, Shep walked Rolex between the aisles, nodding him forward as they reached counsel table. Rolex swaggered toward the bench.

"Sir, please state your full name for the record," the judge said.

With all the lawyers, and now Mr. Rolex, it was close and crowded at the bench.

"Anthony Barthomolu Rolex."

"Would you spell your name for the court reporter?"

"R - O - L—E -X."

"No, I meant your middle name, sir."

Rolex knew what the judge meant; he was trying to warm up to her.

"Thank you. Now please step back, Mr. Rolex. Have a seat in that first row for a moment while I finish some business up here."

"Yes, ma'am."

"So, where are we, counsel? I am aware that it is Ms. Lewis's defense team that located this witness but—"

"Your Honor," Holden interrupted, "we haven't had a chance to speak with this witness."

"That sounds like a problem for the U.S. Attorney's office, not mine," the judge snipped.

Nicki started to jump in. If the issue of Rolex's identification had not come up the way it had, Nicki would have argued her find, her witness, and enabled the record to reflect at least an inference that the prosecutor's office was withholding information it came to be aware of that was helpful to the defense. Under a constitutional case called *Brady*, that's illegal. But Nicki did not want to tip her hand, and she always preferred that the other side be the one getting chewed out by the judge.

"Counsel, I'm going to assume, for your sake, that your office really didn't know where this witness was or what he has to say. That said, since Ms. Lewis' team found the witness first, and you have an obligation to turn over exculpatory evidence to the defense in any regard, Ms. Lewis gets this witness and gets this call."

"But your Hon—"

"Counsel."

"Your Honor, we're just figuring the Mr. Rolex issue out now ourselves," Nicki interrupted, saving the prosecutor from additional harangue from the bench. "We're happy to report back to the court tomorrow on where the defense is on this witness."

"Fine. Step back, counsel," the judge said, and the whole shebang went back to the counsel tables.

"Mr. Rolex, please step up."

Anthony Barthomolu Rolex, wearing jeans, ostrich boots (but no cowboy hat), a black leather jacket, walked up to the bench keeping a warm but professional gaze locked hard on the judge.

"Yes, ma'am."

"Mr. Rolex, I don't know what the defense or the prosecution intends to do with you as a witness, but I am directing you not to leave this city and to remain available."

"Yes, ma'am."

"You understand that this is an order of the court?"

"Yes, ma'am."

"Thank you, step back. The court will likely need you tomorrow so don't go far."

Rolex nodded at the judge, almost imperceptibly—a little nod you would do if you didn't want someone to see you've winked at them—turned on his heels, walked back down the center aisle, and with a hundred eyes trained on him, left the building.

CHAPTER SIX

It was harder for all the lawyers to agree on how Mr. Rolex would appear. After days of wrangling, the defense and prosecution finally resolved that the prosecutor would call him, and the defense would cross-examine. It had been complicated by the fact that one of the alternate jurors lived on the block of the U Street tragedy, did not feel safe staying in the area, and had asked for time to make alternative living arrangements for the duration of the trial. All this took some negotiation and time, but the judge had not minded things slowing down a little bit.

"Mr. Rolex," the AUSA Danny Holden, the prosecutor, began, "can you please tell the court where you were on the evening of August 17th?"

"Yes sir, I can."

"*Would* you please tell the court where you were that evening?"

The prosecutor hoped that the only eyewitness to the crime other than the defendants was not going to make a fool of him on the stand. During preparation for his testimony, Rolex had made it clear that he did not want to testify, especially for the prosecution.

"Yes sir, I will."

Shit, Holden thought, *is he going to make me drag every fact out of him?*

"I was cuttin' tho the alley at F an' 11th—"

"And did you see anything unusual when you were cutting through the alley, Mr. Rolex?" Holden interrupted. He did not want to take the chance of the witness gaining control of the questioning.

"Yeah, I mean, if sometin' unusual is seeing someone gettin' the life beaten out of 'em was unusual, yeah, I would say, yeah. But, if you live in certain parts of this city, no, it wouldn't be no thang, no."

The prosecutor was grateful for the image that Rolex left with the jury—someone getting the life beaten out of them was a terrible picture—but Rolex muddled it up with his mocking, sarcastic tone.

"Mr. Rolex, please describe what you saw that evening in the alley."

AUSA Holden did not want to worsen the exchange he was having with Rolex so he asked what he hoped was a simple enough question the witness would have to answer in a simple enough fashion.

"I saw someone getting the life beaten out of 'em."

"Mr. Rolex," the judge interrupted, "would you please answer the prosecutor's questions?"

Good. I don't have to look like a jerk admonishing my own witness, Holden thought. Nicki looked down from her seat behind the defense table and smiled.

"Yes, ma'am, I will," Rolex said showing the judge the respect he withheld from the prosecutor. "As I began walking through the alley, I saw a commotion, a circle of people, and there was a bunch of movement going on."

"What kind of movement, Mr. Rolex?" the prosecutor asked.

"It looked like three or four guys—beating someone."

"With their fists?" the prosecutor asked.

He knew Mrs. Campbell had been beaten with all kinds of other things too and he wanted the witness to say it—to finish the horrible picture he had begun to paint.

"With their fists, their feet, bats, pipes, anything they could get their hands on."

"And when you came upon this horrible scene, could you tell if Mrs. Campbell was still alive?"

"Objection," Nicki said.

"Sustained."

The judge sounded calm, but she was angered. There is no reason to ask the question that way other than to create sympathy with the jury and it was legally improper. But it was too late. Whatever impression was going to be made on the jury was made. The prosecutor's characterization, the defense objection, the "sustained." They were all out there already.

"I think she was takin' her last breaths," Rolex continued, "You could hear gasping, gulping, sort of, or gurgling, maybe."

Oh my, Nicki thought.

The prosecutor let that impression—the image of a vicious beating, the dreadful sounds of Mrs. Campbell's dying breaths—hang in the air for several seconds before he asked his final question.

"Mr. Rolex, do you see any of the people you saw beating the life out of Mrs. Campbell that night in the courtroom today?"

"Objection," Nicki said, standing.

"Sustained," the judge said in a measured tone. "Watch it, counselor. You well know you are not permitted to characterize a witness' testimony in that manner."

She was purposefully educating the jury and admonishing the prosecutor in front of them, but she knew it was too late. The jury already heard the exchange and they all looked eagerly to Rolex for his answer.

"Mr. Rolex, do you see any of the people you saw that night here in the courtroom today?" Holden corrected.

"Yeah."

"Would you please identify them for the court?"

"I don't know any of 'em," Mr. Rolex said.

He was just about done with the prosecutor as well.

"Yes sir, we know, but would you describe and point out the people you saw that night?"

Rolex was enjoying getting his digs in with the prosecutor. He had always felt that prosecutors especially—like all lawyers—needed to get their comeuppance once in a while because they all thought too mightily of themselves. He had not met a single one who had impressed him. And none of them could fight. Not one of them could protect their families, he believed, and what good was that in a world where what happened to Mrs. Campbell could happen to Mrs. Campbell?

Rolex pointed in the direction of the defendants' table.

"The brother there in the blue suit and white shirt," he began. "The brother next to him in the brown suit and yellow shirt. Ain't see the sister there." And, pointing to the middle of the courtroom, "That dude back there, in the police uniform, but he wasn't wearing that shit that night. Ooops, sorry Your Honor."

Heads spun around in the courtroom. Reporters typed furiously on their phones—a few old schoolers writing in notebooks—and the marshals braced for a commotion. The officer, the subject of all the new excitement, looked straight ahead.

AUSA Holden was on his feet.

"Quiet in the courtroom," Judge Sullivan said bringing down her gavel.

"Approach?" he implored the judge.

Holden had tried to keep his cool, but he was standing over the counsel table with his hands, shoulder-width apart, leaning right into his frustration.

"Chambers, counsel! All of you!" the judge said, bringing the gavel down so hard on her Bible that it left a temporary impression of a circle in the leather. "Bailiff, please take the jury to the jury room. We're on break."

All the defendants were taken to the cellblock behind the bench, and the courtroom sketch artist frantically maneuvered to get a quick rendering of the officer. But in the anarchy and aftermath of Rolex's answer, and all the commotion getting defense counsel up and the jury out, the officer was gone.

"Counsel, do you want to tell me what the hell is going on here?" the judge bellowed at the prosecutor in chambers.

"I don't know, Your Honor. I-I don't know. Mr. Rolex never told me o-or-or any of my investigators about seeing anyone, *anyone*, else in the alley, much less a D.C. Metropolitan Police officer."

Holden had lost control and his voice sounded squeaky and unsteady.

"Counsel, just how many people did Mr. Rolex 'talk to'?" the judge asked with pretend quote fingers.

"Four or five, I think, including me," Holden offered.

"And not one of those four or five, including you, heard anything about this other possible defendant, at least a witness, who happens to be a cop?"

"No, ma'am."

"AUSA Holden, if I have to call every cop and investigator on the force that came within five feet of your witness to find out if he happened to mention it to someone, I will see you brought up on ethics charges and I will seek to preside over your disbarment proceedings."

Judge Sullivan was not known to make idle threats. She was furious.

"Your Honor, maybe the Court should question the witness in chambers," the prosecutor said. He tried to conceal the insult he felt at the judge's insinuation.

"AUSA Holden, I suggest that from this point forward you do not open your mouth to utter a single syllable unless you have heard me explicitly invite you to."

"Your Honor," Nicki interrupted. "Let's just hear him out in chambers. That's what I would suggest, anyway."

Nicki had been on the brutal end of a verbal judicial slaying before, and she knew if it didn't piss you off enough to get yourself held in contempt, it threw your game off. Mostly, though, she wanted a chance to hear what Rolex was talking about.

Judge Sullivan was still angry, but she took a breath and counted to ten in her head. She had learned how well that trick worked years before when she was first appointed and still had the fire and fervor of a judge who was going to make a difference in the criminal justice system. When she was a younger, less experienced judge, Sullivan would permit herself to become personally involved in each matter. In addition to being criticized for it by her judicial evaluators, her early wide-eyed enthusiasm and deep commitment cost her her marriage. Plus, the court reporter was taking notes.

"Marshal, please bring in Mr. Rolex," the judge said through her intercom to Sam Waithe, the head Marshal in her courtroom.

Sam had been around for years, much longer than Judge Sullivan had been, and it was he who had intimated enough about her style on the bench for Judge Sullivan to pursue with her colleagues whether she was too vested in her matters to rule objectively and impartially. It was an awkward conversation, the judge remembered, this big black guy telling this new young, white, female judge that she better cowboy up before she was laughed out of the courthouse. Of course, Sam had not said it that way. He was way too experienced with judges, and too kind, for that. Sam simply "pulled a Sam" as it became known around D.C. Superior Court, telling one of his old stories. When Sam said, "Can I tell you a quick story?" people knew he was about to impart a wisdom that they should heed. Anyway, Sam had helped the judge understand her strengths and weaknesses, and the two of them grew close after that.

"Please take a seat, Mr. Rolex," the judge said as he walked through the chamber's door Sam held open for him with one hand. He kept his other hand on his weapon.

"What's going on, Mr. Rolex?" Judge Sullivan asked.

She did not waste time on the pleasantries she usually imparted to help witnesses feel less nervous in chambers.

"Ma'am?" Rolex asked, "I'm not sure I understand what you mean."

Rolex was not being flip this time. He did not know the lawyers were fighting over the rules about handing over evidence and other proscriptions that can jeopardize the constitutionally required fairness in a criminal trial, and he certainly didn't know what the judge had imputed to the prosecutor.

"Mr. Rolex, you just identified a D.C. Metropolitan police officer as a participant, or at least a witness, in one of the city's most disgusting crimes in more than fifty years. Wanna explain that?"

The judge sounded a bit too facetious, Nicki thought.

"I'm still not sure I understand, but the gentleman I pointed out in the courtroom was in the alley that night. "He," Rolex said pointing to Holden, "asked me if I saw anyone in court who was in the alley that night, and all the men I pointed out in the courtroom were there."

"What was he doing there, Mr. Rolex?" the judge asked.

"He was participating." For several seconds, there was complete silence in the judge's chambers.

"You're telling me that a MPD officer was helping to beat and assault the victim in this case?" the judge asked.

Her calm voice belied the fierce emotions that were raging beneath it.

"Yes, ma'am."

"Thank you, you're excused. Marshal?" the judge said curtly, and suddenly Sam reappeared and escorted Mr. Rolex from chambers. Judge Sullivan didn't buy it.

"With all due respect," Holden said. It had taken him some time to get his jaw up off the floor. "Shouldn't we ask the witness some more questions? I, for one, would like to know whether one of our officers needs to be arrested, among other things."

Nicki started to interject her piece into this preposterous puzzle, but Judge Sullivan was not interested.

"Counsel, we will remain in recess until I call you back. Don't go anywhere," the judge said, and with a sweeping dismissive motion led by her right hand, she signaled the lot of them out of her chambers.

But Judge Sullivan never called the case again that day. The trial was adjourned, and the jury was dismissed. Rolex's bombshells just hung in the air, not really going off, not really landing, not anything. Except at the police department. Rolex's bombshells almost blew the roof off at the MPD.

CHAPTER SEVEN

"What the fuck was that about?" Chief Coley roared at Officer Santiago. "What the Jesus, Mary, and Joseph was that Rolex character talking about? And you better not bullshit me, Miguel, or I'll take your badge right now *and* kick the living shit out of you. I mean it. I will pull your balls out through your asshole."

"I *was* there. Briefly. Undercover. Special assignment from the Feds. I am not supposed to tell you about it. Even if you ever found out."

The police chief had a good relationship with most of the federal guys; he often got a heads-up about confidential investigations when they involved his officers even when other police chiefs did not. But he had nothing on this.

"Miguel, my phone started ringing off the damned hook from the second Rolex fingered you," Coley bellowed. "What the hell am I going to say—that Officer Miguel was executing his duty as an officer and in no way was engaged in causing Mrs. Campbell harm? You know what the next questions are? What the hell kind of duty would permit a police officer to watch a 55-year-old grandmother get the shit beaten out of her from the inside out? What the fuck? Don't we have enough going on with that U Street horror show?"

"I'm not sure what you want me—"

The chief's office phone rang, interrupting their clash.

"Don't move!" Coley said to Miguel, snatching up his cell phone.

Miguel was relieved for the reprieve—maybe the Mayor was calling—but either way, he was hoping not to have to keep lying to his boss.

"*What*?!" Coley yelled into the phone.

"Jim? David," Agent Stackhouse said.

The police chief motioned for Miguel to get out of his office, slammed the door behind him, and drew the blinds.

CHAPTER EIGHT

The press was divided between its focus on a local murder, albeit atrocious, and the high-level intrigue of the U Street investigation. There had been little talk about U Street outside the precinct—no significant leaks that Chief Coley could verify—so the newspapers ran the same headlines over and over: "Scene So Grisly Veteran Officer Vomits," "Horrible Human Remains Discovered in Back Room."

What the press didn't know would have produced headlines only Hollywood could invent, Coley knew, and he had no doubt in his mind that, legal or not, his decision to shut down the information flow was right. Plus, he had other things to worry about.

"How's it going?" he asked CC.

The crime lab folks had been working nonstop for seventeen days. They were working in shifts. The task was daunting, and members of the team were quitting regularly now for "mental health reasons." CC was on auto-pilot. She methodically categorized, tested, and analyzed every drop and scrap of evidence they collected. It took thirteen days just to finish processing the inside of the house; by day six the crime scene investigators had discovered enough different blood types they thought they might never know how many victims were involved, and of those, how many might be still living, or dead.

"I have no idea how to answer that question," CC responded with a sigh. "We're tired. We're not through. One pool of blood sample we analyzed comprised different types of metal."

"What do you mean?" Coley had been so tense lately that many of his questions came out like accusations.

"What do I mean? I mean the poor son-of-a-bitch who belongs—or belonged—to that blood was tortured or stabbed by different types of metal instruments. Maybe a knife, another kind of knife, maybe a—"

"I get it, I get it."

"And remember last Tuesday when I told you I wasn't sure if we'd ever know how many victims there were and whether they are all dead or some still alive?"

"Yeah?"

"Well, so far we've identified the DNA of five separate and distinct individuals. Two the exact same. Two the exact same. And one ... well, mixture," CC said.

"What are you talking about?" Coley felt a knot in his stomach like nothing he'd known in all his years as a cop.

"Two adults. Two children, all ... clones, it appears. And one human/animal clone combination."

"Human clones? Here? In America?"

Like many people who followed the news reports about the progress of cloning, Coley assumed the Chinese would be the first to clone a human being. He figured that without the moral, social, and legal proscriptions against human cloning that exist in the U.S., the Chinese could be pretty far along by now. The possibility that the U.S. might be involved in human cloning astounded him. He wanted to ask CC what type of animal made up the human/animal combination, but he couldn't bring himself to do it. Mostly though, he couldn't fathom how CC could be talking about it so calmly.

"Remember the remains we found that we couldn't really identify?" CC answered. "The small-sized head compared to the body that seemed to go with it? The extra fingers? The weird looking feet? We think someone cloned a baby with a pig. We heard a rumor about a top-secret NIH and Energy Department test program going on under the Secret Service, but that doesn't make any sense, of course. It's probably just a rumor. They're all kinds of wild rumors about all this."

Coley groaned and headed for the door. Before swiping his identification card to exit, he looked back at CC. "We're in the goddam Twilight Zone, CC."

She smiled, weakly, but when the thick steel doors clanged their final, locked clack, she said to no one in particular, "You don't know the half of it."

Agent Stackhouse could see the strain on Coley's face, not that Stackhouse looked so hot himself. It was a pretty day, though. Spring was not far off now—the best time of the year in the nation's capital, when the cherry blossom trees around the Tidal Basin were in bloom. In addition to the historical significance, and beauty of the trees, they keep secrets. All kinds of things have happened under them. It is where the big defense contractors swapped top secret Defense Department specs back in the eighties, causing the court martial of top military brass, the convictions of nine DOD contractors, twenty guilty pleas, one suicide, one possible suicide, and a plethora of congressional hearings. It's where Agent Stackhouse sometimes went to find peace. Or to meet people. It's where the President first learned about Abby. And Area 51.

It was nice there in the fall too, though when the leaves died and fell, secrets often did as well. Anyway, it wasn't quite spring yet, but the air hinted it was around the corner, and that was good for lots of reasons. For one, it would mean that Mrs. Campbell's case would be over and U street probably petering out. For now, though, both cases were weeks in, and at least one of them had miles to go and secrets to keep.

"How you doin', man?" Agent Stackhouse said, shaking Coley's hand.

"Okay. You?"

"Fine, fine."

"Just checking in, I guess. Our last call was so brief."

Coley was hoping Agent Stackhouse would give him something.

"It is what it is. How's your team doing?"

"The crime lab guys are all going to go insane I suspect, if not from the non-stop work then from the forensics they're seeing."

"Yeah. Pretty nasty stuff."

Agent Stackhouse almost always held things close to his vest. His thoughts, his emotions, his views on most things. Not surprising for a Secret Service agent, to be sure, but David Stackhouse might have come into the world that way. Or maybe the world imposed it on him in some manner, some time ago.

"Aren't givin' up anything, huh?" Coley chuckled.

"What would you like, my friend, my ol' buddy, my pal?" Stackhouse laughed back.

"Well, just what you guys think is really going on at U Street. Who did this? Why?"

Agent Stackhouse had been mulling over when to bring Police Chief Coley in the loop. He trusted him—that wasn't the issue. The issue was how big of a secret it was. What it could mean if it spilled out. What it could mean if it spilled out even accidentally. Most importantly, it wasn't his secret to share. It was the President's.

"It's like the salt flats in Bolivia."

Agent Stackhouse decided against it.

"What are you talking about, Stack?" Coley chuckled.

He was happy to see they were getting into an old, warm, familiar space, where he could call his friend by his nickname as his friend wandered off about some arcane fact or observation.

"I'm talking about the mirror-like Salar de Uyuni salt flat in Bolivia. In pictures, it looks like a shiny, flat reflective solid surface but in reality, it's a salt flat."

"Again, what are you talking about?" Coley rolled his eyes.

"Okay, what are you, six years old?" Stackhouse laughed. "You're not just pedestrian, you're juvenile. It's a metaphor. That what we're seeing isn't what we're seeing."

"I know what a metaphor is, Stack." Coley laughed back. "I just wanted to see how all professor you'd go on me. You didn't disappoint."

Stackhouse smiled, looked out on the Potomac for a while, then down at his feet so the movement of his lips would be shielded from interpretation.

"Don't know yet."

"Really?" Coley was partly relieved that this top, world-class agency had not come up with anything.

"Would you tell me if you knew anything?"

"I would tell you, but not before I told POTUS," Stackhouse said, referring to President Pierce.

Coley thought it was interesting that the President didn't know anything yet. Either there really was nothing yet to know, or Stackhouse knew something and just had not had a chance to tell the President about it. Of course, Coley knew the Secret Service always has access to the President—they can tell him anything they want, anytime they want, if they need to. *If the President doesn't know yet, maybe there really is nothing yet to know,* he thought.

"Let's head back, Jim," Agent Stackhouse said.

As they walked the path at the west end of the Tidal Basin, where their meeting protocol would send them in different directions, Coley's phone rang.

The last time a phone rang on their way back, it was Stack's, Coley remembered.

"What's up, C?" Sometimes Coley called Cecilia just the one "C," which Cecilia had figured out over time was a sign of affection or endearment.

"Nothing good. We discovered the blood of victim number seven."

"I'm sorry," Coley said.

"It's definitely Sheila's niece. It's confirmed."

Cecilia's voice was barely audible, and Coley almost dropped the phone. As he grabbed it with his right hand, he reached out to Stackhouse with his left.

"David," Coley said quietly, "they found enough of Abby's blood to believe she's dead."

He waited for David to get on his phone, call for a car, ask more questions—anything. Instead, he said, "I told you we didn't have anything, Chief."

Agent Stackhouse sounded irritated now, which confused Coley. He did not know what game Stackhouse was playing, but he *did* know that three top-secret federal government labs did not get important information wrong. He knew their results had to be reliable, and now he was angry that after all these years his old friend would not tell him what was going on.

But Agent Stackhouse had already walked away, and left Coley standing there. Again.

Coley had meetings back at the precinct, but he went to see Cecilia instead. He was unsettled when he got to the lab. He was looking for answers.

"Didn't expect to see you in person, Chief. But thanks for coming by."

"What can you tell me about the findings? How sure are we?"

"I don't know how much surer we can be. Understanding the consequences of it, we have gone over this time and again. Is there an issue?"

"No issue, just some contrary information," Coley said, "though I'm not sure I believe it."

"I can walk you through the science if you like."

Coley had anticipated that CC would make such an offer—that's why he had hesitated before heading there. If she walked him through the science, and there really appeared to be no doubt about the President's daughter Abby's DNA, how was he supposed to think about what Agent Stackhouse had told him (three times now)? He did not want to believe it was Abby's DNA anyway, for lots of obvious reasons. But he truly could not accept the fact that his long-time friend Stack could look right at him and lie straight to his face.

"Nah. You have enough to do," Coley said to Cecilia. "You didn't need me interfering with your work, as tough as it is already."

Coley knew CC would not buy that, but also that she wouldn't push it.

"Well, you know where to find me if you change your mind. You know I don't mind, Chief. Who knows, maybe going through the exercise again will turn up something we missed."

"I know you don't mind. I'm good. Thank you. I'll check in with you later."

"You got it."

Coley was right. Cecilia didn't buy it. But she wasn't going to push it.

CHAPTER NINE

"Will the court please come to order," the clerk said, calling the case again after all the delays. Everyone who had been milling about started to take their seats.

"The court is now in session. Judge Sullivan presiding."

"Ladies and gentlemen of the jury," the judge started. "When we were last together, well, the day ended in an eventful manner. You might have noticed."

Some of the jurors smiled meekly. Judge Sullivan was trying to ease the jurors' tension and remove the pall that still hung over the courtroom from Mr. Rolex identifying a MPD officer as someone he saw at Mrs. Campbell's crime scene, and it seemed to be working.

"It was like a scene on *N.Y.P.D.*, or *Judge Judy*, or one of those shows like that, huh? Well, remember at the beginning of the trial, I told you that sometimes during a trial, things can happen that can cause an interruption or cause counsel and me to meet here at the bench or even in chambers?"

The jurors nodded; a few quietly said yes.

"Well, that happened yesterday during Mr. Rolex's testimony. Mr. Rolex is going to get back on the stand and finish his testimony today, but he will only be speaking about the defendants in this case. It was not appropriate for him to have referred to anyone in this case except for those who are charged and sitting at counsel table, and that part of his testimony will be stricken from the record. You are not to consider that aspect of Mr. Rolex's testimony in any manner whatsoever, do you understand?"

Most of the jurors nodded, but while the judge's instructions were going on, Nicki noticed the court reporter was not taking notes—she had not recorded a single thing the judge had said. In the more than fifty cases Nicki had tried, not once had she seen the court reporter deliberately fail to take notes. *What is going on?*

"Mr. Prosecutor, please re-call your witness," the judge continued.

As soon as the judge spoke the words "please re-call your witness" Nicki noticed, the court reporter began taking notes again. Nicki scribbled her own note and handed it behind her, over the railing that separates counsel table from the audience seats, to Shep: "FIND OUT WHAT THE FUCK IS GOING ON!"

"Mr. Rolex, yesterday you testified that the defendants sitting at the table were involved in the savage beating," AUSA Holden said taking up where he'd left off.

"Objection," Nicki said. The other defendants' lawyers noted their objections as well.

"Sustained," Judge Sullivan said quickly.

"I said all but the female. I did not see her there," Mr. Rolex said.

In all the other days' confusion, no one noticed that Mr. Rolex had specifically exculpated Nicki's client. Except Nicki.

"Yes," the prosecutor said, irritated.

"Are you absolutely certain you saw each of these men in the alley that night?"

"Yes sir. Each of the men."

"And you saw each of these men individually beating Mrs. Campbell?"

"Careful, counsel," the judge interrupted.

"Yes. How many times do you want me to say it?" Rolex replied impatiently.

Nicki was glad she had made the strategic decision to have Rolex be the prosecutor's witness. He was not an easy one to examine, and he looked like a thug. Let the prosecutor have to deal with his credibility issues, she thought. Still, no one seemed to know what was going on with his identification of a police officer, other than the obvious possibility that he was undercover; and that didn't explain the court reporter's behavior. What did the judge know that would make it okay for a court reporter not to record the proceedings? *A national security issue might explain something like that,* Nicki thought; this was Washington, after all. But there was no possibility on the planet that a bunch of criminals beating up a grandmother in Southeast D.C. could relate to national security. No way.

When it was Nicki's turn to cross-examine Rolex, she decided to introduce some lightness into the courtroom. The jury was relieved when the judge had done it earlier, and Nicki's cross-examination was going to be short anyway. Her only objective was to unequivocally reinforce that the one eyewitness to this crime said her client wasn't there. That, and not having him go off again and say something spectacularly unhelpful. Short and sweet. In and out.

"Good morning, Mr. Rolex. How're you feeling today?" Nicki began.

"Very very fine, thank you," Mr. Rolex answered. He sat up straighter in his seat, smoothed his tie. He looked like he was trying to impress Nicki.

"I don't have many questions, but I have a couple, and I'll try to ask them directly, so the judge doesn't get mad at me and the prosecutor doesn't jump out of his seat." It was a cheap shot at Holden, but it made the jury laugh. The judge looked down at her papers so the jury would not see her smiling.

Yes! Nicki high-fived herself, in her head.

"Okay, Mr. Rolex, the prosecutor asked you whether you were absolutely certain you saw these men in the alley that evening, and you said you were certain, correct?"

"Yes, ma'am."

"You also testified you were certain my client, Ms. Gray was not in the alley—is that correct, Mr. Rolex?"

"Yes, ma'am. Your client was not at the scene."

"Well, thank you very much, Mr. Rolex, for taking the time to come to court and tell the truth," Nicki said.

It was a completely gratuitous and improper remark, but the prosecutor could not risk another confrontation with his own witness, so he didn't object. The lawyers for the other defendants did though, but Nicki didn't care about that now.

"Don't you want to know how I—"

"You're excused, Mr. Rolex," the judge interrupted. Judge Sullivan thought Rolex was going to ignore the instructions she gave him about what was permissible to talk about and what wasn't, and she really didn't want a repeat of the prior courtroom drama. But he was going to say something else altogether.

"Yes, ma'am," Rolex answered, and he left the stand, keeping his other big secret.

CHAPTER TEN

"Mr. President, thank you for seeing me," Agent Stackhouse said.

President Clifford Scott Pierce was the youngest and, arguably, brightest president in modern American history—a truth that was fairly-widely undisputed, even by his detractors. He was tall and handsome and physically imposing. His shoulders were straight and broad, he had large hands with long fingers, and he kept his weight college-adjacent by playing basketball, boxing, and mountain-climbing—all of which the Secret Service hated. A twisted ankle playing ball could be explained, they figured. Getting decked in the ring? Not as much, they knew.

"Hi, Abby."

The President's daughter Abby Cooper was coloring on a couch in the Oval Office. Agent Stackhouse thought the Oval somehow had the capacity to embrace with warmth a child playing, while also convey the gravity of its purpose, the weight of its history. Agent Stackhouse mostly felt the gravity part.

"Hi, Mr. Secret Agent Man!" Abby squeaked.

When Abby was younger, her mother watched reruns of the decades-old TV show and Abby had been calling Special Agent Stackhouse "Mr. Secret Agent Man" ever since. Agent Stackhouse thought it was adorable, but he pretended he was chagrined each time she did it, he frowned up his face in feigned vexation. That made Abby giggle even more, almost uncontrollably, and the President delighted in the whole scene, no matter how many times they played it out, and today he indulged himself longer than usual in their little game.

"Abby," he finally said, "Agent Stackhouse and I need to talk about grown-up stuff."

Abby jumped up and skipped out through a door that looked like a wall.

"See you later alligator, Secret Agent Man," she squealed.

President Pierce loved Abby. She was beautiful. Olive-skinned with long wavy brown hair, almond-shaped eyes, near perfect features. She was warm, bubbly, affectionate, and smart. He desperately wanted people to know about her.

To everything there is a season, and a time to every purpose under heaven, he told himself when he felt wistful about his secret family.

"David, I appreciate your warmth toward Abby."

"Yes, sir, you've told me."

"I don't want you to forget it."

"She's delightful, Mr. President."

"Yes, yes, she is."

The President's voice trailed off as he looked out the French doors over the South Lawn.

President Pierce struggled mightily with the arrangement he had made with Sheila. For now, at Abby's tender age of four, it worked. Soon though, he and Sheila knew, they would have to explain who Sheila really was to her. He worried constantly about whether they never should have begun the ruse, and what it would do to Abby's young psyche when she found out.

"Mr. President," Agent Stackhouse said pulling the President back from his wistfulness.

"We're going to have to make a move on U Street."

"I assume it's unavoidable?"

"Yes, sir. Police Chief Coley has done a very good job keeping the lid on it, but we could not interrupt the normal investigative processes without inviting questions and the science—well, you're aware."

"Keep me posted," the President said.

Such an ordinary, everyday expression for such an extraordinary, unprecedented set of events. Agent Stackhouse left through yet another door that looked like a wall.

Leading up to and throughout his campaign for the presidency, some of his top advisors—long seasoned political operatives—shared with him that the rumors about some of the grim things presidents were called upon—to do, to authorize, to oversee—were true. That presidents throughout time had sanctioned some of the most dreadful actions in human history in order to preserve or protect our way of life. It went way beyond sending young men and women to war. And while he remained stalwart in those briefings, some of the historical examples he was told turned his stomach and made him think long and hard about whether he could make such a call if required and, more importantly, whether he could live with himself afterwards. In the end, he held out hope that nothing would happen on his watch that would require such an analysis and judgment call. But he learned, in just his first year, how pie-in-the-sky that thinking was, and to his surprise and dismay, how often the damn question came up. He also learned what that sort of power meant—how it could be used for the greater good—as never before.

"Yes, sir. Have a good evening, sir," Stackhouse said. But he knew it would not be a good evening.

Around 12:30 a.m. that night, sirens screamed as the fire trucks raced the wrong way up U Street. Initially a four-alarm fire, it quickly became a seven alarm, then an eight, then a ten. The flames leaped so high it was impossible that nearby houses wouldn't catch. And there was that hideous smell.

The assistant fire chief yelled into the two-way, "I don't know what's going on here. I've never seen—or smelled anything like it."

"What do you mean 'smell?'" the fire chief answered.

"Better come down."

At the police precinct, Coley was screaming into the phone, too.

"What, what, I can't hear you?"

"U Street's burnin', Chief."

"Shit! I'll be right there—Rick, CC," Chief Coley yelled, "let's go!"

"What's going on?" CC said as the police chief's unmarked car raced through downtown D.C. She had just finished another update meeting with Coley and was headed back to her temporary digs near the Chief when she heard him calling after her. She could hear the radio chatter and make out that there was an enormous fire at U Street.

Agent Stackhouse had not been returning Coley's phone calls lately—something that had troubled him—and when Coley and his team got to the scene, Coley was certain the fire was no accident. It raged so hot it was impossible to get close enough to douse it. And it was exceedingly precise. The flames rose straight up, yet there were few sparks. Dozens of firefighters remarked about the intensity and exactness of the blaze. It was sure to end up in training videos and film—no question.

"Chief," Coley nodded to the fire chief.

"Coley," the fire chief nodded back. "Do you know anything about this?"

"Nothing that I can share."

"Shit, Coley. What do you mean nothing you can share? Look at that thing! How am I supposed to explain why forty-seven firefighters stood by watching a house in the middle of the city burn to the ground? And we already had to arrest some pinhead around the back trying to get close enough to get pictures of the inside. God knows what he's got in his camera. Dammit, you have got to give me some—"

The fire chief's phone rang, interrupting his rant.

He held a finger up to Coley and walked away from the trucks and the noise. Squeezing his left ear in, he held the phone tight against the right one, "Fire Chief Ramsey."

"Chief?" Ramsey's face turned from frustration to gravity. "It's David."

All night long local news stations interrupted primetime shows to repeat the same initial feed about the fire:

> "Firefighters stood by helplessly as this house on U Street, just blocks from the White House, burned so fiercely they could not get near it. An unidentified noxious odor was so strong the fire chief determined it a hazmat zone, ordered his firefighters back, and they all just watched as the house literally burned to the ground. There is nothing left of the building, as you can see behind me. There appear to be mounds of ash but there is no debris. No remnants at all of what was in that house. No one this reporter spoke to can explain the fire burning so hot, so precisely, and so completely. Gwen Joyner, *ABC News*"

There was no doubt about it in Coley's mind, though. Some agency of the United States government had deliberately set the fire. And his old buddy Stack knew all about it.

When the fire chief rejoined Coley's team, he did not ask Coley any more questions about what he did or didn't know. Instead, he made a suggestion.

"Coley, why don't we do a joint press conference and get this over with?"

"And say what?" Coley asked.

It was obvious to Coley that the phone call that pulled Fire Chief Rick Ramsey away in the middle of their conversation was revealing, and just as obvious that Ramsey wasn't going to share it with him.

"That this appears to be a complicated investigation with several agencies working together, and that when we have something to report, we will do so. Something like that," Ramsey responded.

"And what about the crime scene processing we had been doing?" CC interjected.

"Well, that's over," Ramsey snapped. "Don't you think?" he said, softening.

"What do you mean it's over? We can still process what's left. Maybe there's more evidence now that the structure's been, well, deconstructed," CC said.

"I'm sorry Cecelia, the fire department will be declaring the site hazardous, and it will not be able to be processed further."

"I don't know what all this cloak and dagger shit is all about but I'm sick of it," Coley said. "Say whatever the hell you want, Chief, but I'm out of it."

Ramsey didn't blame Police Chief Coley. He was not able to share what he had just been directed in his phone call, even with Coley, who had been a good colleague and friend through the years (including when they were rising in their respective departments in D.C.). Ramsey knew he would feel the same way if the tables were turned. But the press conference would not go well if the police department was absent. More importantly, the instructions he got on that call were clear—Fire Chief Ramsey and Police Chief Coley were to do the press conference together.

"I need you to do me a solid on this one, Jim."

Ramsey hoped the use of one of their old school expressions would warm Coley to it, though he knew their situation was too serious for informality. He didn't know what else to do. Agent Stackhouse had been clear. Fire Chief Ramsey looked straight into Police Chief Coley's eyes as he waited for the man's response.

"Goddammit, Rick," Coley said.

A few minutes later, the pair of chiefs stood in front of the surging press.

"Ladies and gentlemen, if you could settle down," the fire chief's aide said into the microphones.

There are an awful lot of microphones for a house fire, Chief Ramsey thought, *even a big one.*

Fifty or more reporters had gathered back at the fire station on less than thirty minutes notice. Chief Ramsey stepped up to the microphones and began.

"Ladies and gentlemen, unfortunately this will be extremely brief. We will not be taking questions right now. Currently, all I can say is that this is a complicated and multi-jurisdictional matter. Several agencies—"

"Which agencies?" a reporter in the front interrupted.

"As I said, we will not be taking questions at this time," Ramsey continued.

"How about you, Chief Coley?" another reporter asked.

"As soon as the agencies that are working together on this coordinate a little further, we will come back to you with what we can. I'm sorry," Chief Ramsey said, looking from the first reporter to the second.

"That's all at this time," Coley agreed.

He was not happy. Somebody was trying to burn his city down, literally and figuratively. And all he could do was be a parrot. Something that was neither his style nor his reputation. And one of his closest friends in the world, Stack, had turned out to be a big fat liar.

"There is a rumor that there were several murders in this house a week or so ago. Can anyone address that *currently*?" a reporter from the back yelled.

Both Coley and Ramsey had been around long enough not to show their hands when a reporter asked a question that hit on something they could not or did not choose to talk about, so neither of them did (despite the upward drone of discontent).

"One more time," Ramsey said quietly, "we will not be taking questions, *currently*."

He could be sarcastic too. And he turned away from the microphones just in time to catch Agent Stackhouse give him a nod and slip out a side door of the fire station, unnoticed by the crowd, except for Coley.

For six days after the fire, hazmat guys in space suits took readings from the site every few hours, and the Environmental Protection Agency officially declared the area toxic and uninhabitable. Bureau of Alcohol, Tobacco, Firearms and Explosives was there. The Department of Energy was there, too, for some reason. And someone swore they saw men with NASA engineer patches on their jackets.

Four families who lived in nearby homes were evacuated—two families on each side. Seventeen people in all, including the reclusive guy on the corner who literally never spoke to anyone and rarely left his home.

No one knew what the recluse did, and he dressed mysteriously, often in black. His home looked immaculate from the outside; his yard was perennially and impeccably manicured, and he always set out exactly one small can of trash on collection day, retrieving it the moment the sanitation workers emptied it. No one recalled ever seeing any kind of delivery to his house, not pizza or Chinese food, or packages. Did he even get any mail?

No one even knew his name. If they weren't already overwhelmed by all that was going on at U Street, the police might have investigated him just because he was so weird. The neighborhood was buzzing with conspiracy theories about his involvement in the fire. When the authorities knocked on mystery man's door and told him he had to leave his home for at least several weeks, and that the federal government was going to pay for him to stay in a nice hotel during that time, he didn't ask any questions. He just packed a small bag and went where they told him.

One of the MPD officers wrote in his notepad that he should circle back and talk with mystery man further. But he never did. The MPD did not have the time or the resources with everything that was going on, and mystery man never went back to his house, even after he was cleared to. Someone came every week and gardened, put out the bags of leaves when they fell, a single trash can, waited for the trash trucks to come, and then took the can back in.

After the fire, things quieted down a little for Police Chief Coley. Reporters had such trouble getting any real information that many of them moved on to other stories. A few were still poking around, trying to learn something they could scoop, but most just filed their notes among the other dead-enders and kept an ear out. Nice for Coley. He was exhausted. Both the work, and the emotions he was dealing with, had worn him down. He drank more than usual at night—he was having trouble ridding his mind of the images from inside U Street before it blew up. That's how people described it now—less a fire than an explosion. Maybe some sort of gas explosion, people began to say, though that idea had been deliberately planted, and the gas company adamantly denied it.

CHAPTER ELEVEN

A few days after the U Street fire, and weeks now since the trial for Mrs. Campbell's murder began, the prosecutor rested his case. Nicki thought Holden had done a decent job, but he had not touched her client. In fact, he may have made her case for her, especially with Rolex's testimony. Still, there was always the danger with the jury that if she did nothing in defense of the charges but cross-examine the prosecutor's witnesses—a right the law explicitly recognizes—the jury could assign blame to her client's silence. Of course, not having her client testify was not the same thing as not putting on a defense at all.

Nicki drank too much that night. It was a hard existence representing indigent men and women charged with horrible crimes. It was as dirty and gritty and emotionally draining as anything she could do, and few appreciated the hard work and sacrifice and danger—not even the clients. This case was one of the dirtiest, and all kinds of unexpected things kept happening. Things she did not understand.

Still, she had to figure it out.

"I don't know what the hell to do," Nicki said to Stoli, her cat, as she poured a third glass of wine. "Yeah I do," she said as she nestled into her favorite work chair, Stoli curling up beside her. She had to put on some kind of a defense, whether that included her client's testimony or not. As good as she was at cross-examination, she didn't feel comfortable having all of the other defendants' lawyers put on a defense without her own. She loved being in front of a jury, and while cross-examinations put you in front of the jury, they didn't do it the same way putting on your own witnesses did. Putting on your own case meant telling your side of the story, on your terms, Nicki knew. She knew that even though the law requires juries *not* to read anything negative into a defendant choice—and the judge gives them strict instructions about how everyone is presumed innocent, yada, yada—they always do. Nicki had experienced it time and time again. Criminal juries always assume that a defendant who doesn't testify is a guilty defendant.

It took a week for the other defendants' lawyers to finish putting on their respective cases, a hodgepodge of misidentification and bad science, enough to raise the question of reasonable doubt (they hoped), especially after Rolex's testimony. Their hope was to muddy the waters of the overall case, take the focus from Rolex, and enable them to convince the jury in closing arguments that there were too many open questions for them to convict their clients of a crime, albeit atrocious, that carried a life sentence. The crime deserved that, no question. Mrs. Campbell deserved no less, they wanted to lay the foundation for the rightful defendants. Muddying the waters was key to that. Taking the focus from Rolex and his testimony was crucial.

"Ms. Lewis, please call your first witness," the judge said when it was finally Nicki's turn to begin the defense of her client.

The courtroom was full again, especially with the news draught on U Street.

Most of the reporters from the first days of the trial were back, along with a few new ones. Because it was the defendants turn to put on their cases, more family members were in attendance, for the defendants and for Mrs. Campbell. It was just short of the marshal service calling for overflow protocols where audience members had to stage in a separate room and watch the trial via live video feed. Shep swept the room with his normal gaze, always looking out for any trouble. Things looked typical enough; he'd nodded to Nicki before she stood up.

"The defense calls Mr. Rolex, Your Honor," Nicki said, though she hardly got the words out before the prosecutor was on his feet.

"OBJECTION!"

AUSA Holden's pitch was so severe it caused the jurors' heads to reel around as if they had heard a gun go off.

"Approach," the judge said sternly to the lawyers. "Ms. Lewis, you better have a good explanation."

"I do, Your Honor."

It took a few seconds for all the defendants' lawyers to squeeze together at the bench. Two of them dagger-eyed Nicki.

"As you know, there is no case that restricts a defendant from re-calling a witness if the witness is still available and willing to appear," Nicki said. "And since Mr. Rolex was the prosecutor's witness, we do not have a 'notice' problem."

"You had a chance to cross-examine this witness during the prosecutor's case, Ms. Lewis, and given the explosive nature of his testimony previously, I can't think of a reason on this earth that I would give you another bite at this apple. Not one!"

The judge did not want another disruption like the last one, nor did she want to deal with all the legal issues that arose the last time Rolex was on the stand. She certainly did not want anything else to happen that could lend support to a mistrial. This was the nastiest, most gruesome case she had seen in a long time, and she did not want to have to try it more than once.

"Your Honor," Nicki continued, "since the prosecutor failed to inform counsel of this witness' knowledge that my client was not at the scene—something that otherwise would be grounds for a mistrial had not Mr. Rolex testified under oath to her absence from the scene—there can be no objection from counsel, and I am asking the court's barest, minimalist indulgence with this witness," Nicki said. "I am certain the relevance of Mr. Rolex's testimony for the defendant will be clear in minutes."

AUSA Holden was seething. "My strenuous objection stands, Your Honor."

Judge Sullivan was not happy. But the prospect of having to re-try this case because of a mistrial, even for one witness, was unthinkable. Better to indulge Ms. Lewis a little with lots of admonitions.

"Ms. Lewis, I am going to give you just enough rope to hang yourself on this one and I mean it," Judge Sullivan snarled. "I'm telling you, if the relevancy of this witness's testimony doesn't bound from his lips within minutes of him sitting down, you and I are going to have a very difficult conversation about where you will be spending the night."

That's a pretty strong threat of being held over in contempt of court, Nicki thought. It made the whole court-reporter-not-recording-the-jury-instructions-about-Mr. Rolex's-testimony-thing even more curious. And all of it made the prosecutor fume. And also, nervous.

The marshal in the front nodded to the marshal in the back to get Mr. Rolex. Rolex was sitting on a bench outside the courtroom scrolling through messages on his phone. He didn't know how long all this was going to take and he wanted to return any urgent texts before he had to turn off his phone and step into the courtroom for the second time. The first time, he had caused a bit of a stir.

After the judge re-instructed the jury regarding the prior appearance of Mr. Rolex, Nicki got up, walked around counsel table, semi-sat against the front of the table, and interlaced her fingers of both hands then let them fall relaxed against her lap. Shep looked down and smiled. Nicki had a few courtroom stances—this was his favorite.

"Mr. Rolex," Nicki began, "I am going to ask the court reporter to read back your testimony from the last time you were here, and ask you to tell the court whether that is indeed what you said, okay?"

"Yes, ma'am."

"Mrs. Spencer," Nicki said to the court reporter, "would you please read back Mr. Rolex's previous testimony?"

Nicki always took care to learn the names of the court reporters and to address them politely and respectfully. It was the right thing to do given the hard work and long hours they put in, and it paid the dividend of getting early transcripts in a pinch.

Mrs. Spencer wasn't sure if Nicki really meant her to read the entire testimony, but she liked Nicki and she'd been around long enough to have a good sense of what to do; she flipped back through the transcript to what Rolex had said about Nicki's client.

"Now, Mr. Rolex, you seemed awfully certain that my client Ms. Gray was not at the scene, did not participate, had nothing whatsoever to do with Mrs. Campbell's horrible death," Nicki said, leading the witness.

"Objection!" The prosecutor was on his feet again, face beet purple. "Object to the characterization, Your Honor!"

It was a stupid objection given his own improper characterizations previously, and not even the right one. Nicki tried not to roll her eyes.

"Are you sure, Mr. Prosecutor? Are you saying you wouldn't characterize Mrs. Campbell's death as horrible, given that you characterized it the exact same way previously?" the judge asked.

"Of course, of course, but I was objecting to the context and/or implication Ms. Lewis was making." Holden knew it was a bad call as soon as the words came out, and the judge knew what he really meant. He was overreacting to what he didn't know the witness might say or what Nicki was after, and Judge Sullivan, well, she was just messing with him.

"Proceed, Ms. Lewis."

"Mrs. Spencer, would you please read back the question?" Nicki asked.

Everybody knew the question. It was a cheap trick really, to rub it in, to give the offending question added legitimacy by having the words officially read back from the transcript. But it usually worked when Nicki did it.

"Ms. Lewis let's not get out of hand," the judge interrupted, slowing down the head of steam Nicki was trying to build up.

"Your Honor, if you don't mind, I'd like to hear it again," Mr. Rolex said. He might as well have outright winked at Nicki.

As the court reporter read back the question, the jurors were all watching Mr. Rolex, anxiously waiting to hear whether his answer would be the same from the days before and what would happen if it weren't.

"I know that your client Ms. Gray was not there because I was there, and she wasn't," Mr. Rolex said.

Not that helpful, Nicki thought. *That wasn't really different or better than what he'd said previously. Maybe I made the wrong call on this one.*

Nicki let that question roll around in her head for just a second before she snapped herself out of it.

Of course, it was the right call.

Last time Rolex made an identification it had caused a bit of a stir and it wasn't clear to Nicki that that important fact had registered sufficiently with the jury. Shep had agreed when Nicki talked to him about it. If Nicki could get Rolex to be really clear and specific, she might have a real chance of her client being dismissed out of the case. He was still a fact witness—something the jury could debate about—but his testimony upped the chances for her client.

"I also know," Rolex continued, "because I had just—"

But just then the sirens that had been singing quietly in the background of the courthouse periodically through most of the trial were suddenly screaming. They were screaming so loud that the microphones in the courtroom were not strong enough to amplify the courtroom voices and drown out the sirens' urgency. Abruptly and unexpectedly U.S. Marshals and police officers suddenly scurried Judge Sullivan out of the courtroom, protecting her with their bodies and their guns; the lawyers, the witness, court personnel and jurors all were being dashed through back and side doors of the courtroom.

"Oh my God, what's happening?!" someone yelled as the first shots rang out.

The courtroom turned from controlled confusion to complete chaos. The galleries, packed with spectators every day since the newsworthy trial began again, became a melee of screaming men and women, pushing, shoving, ducking for cover. Shep threw his body over Nicki's, scooped her up as if she carried only the weight of a child, and scurried them both through one of the side doors. The uproar did not stop until the rapid-fire gun shots did and when it was over, thirteen people were dead, including a juror.

"Shep!"

That was the only word Nicki could find to speak, but she didn't need to say anymore.

"I know, I know," he tried to assure. "Do you want me to get you out of here before the police lock us all down for questioning?"

As officers of the court, it would have been an inappropriate thing to do at best; for Nicki, possibly a violation of the D.C. Bar rules. Shep didn't care.

"No, no," Nicki got out. She was calming down now, finding comfort in the logic of rules and regulations. "Let's see if we can find out what's happening. God—do you think it's related to the trial?"

And now, Nicki was no longer calm.

"With everything that's going on in this trial, in the city, you have to consider it," Shep responded.

"Counsel?" an MPD officer said, having found them around the corner from the courtroom in a back hallway. "Are you all right? Are you hurt?'

"Yes? I mean, no, I'm not hurt. I'm fine. Fine."

"Very good. We'll need to get a statement, of course."

"Of course."

"Sir? Are you with Ms. Lewis?"

"Yes, sir. Ray Shepherd. I'm an investigator for the Public Defender Service."

"We'll definitely need your statement then, too, Mr. Shepherd."

"Call me Shep."

"Thank you for your cooperation."

"Anything you can tell us? I know it's early but . . . " Shep was trying to establish a rapport with the officer, find out what the early buzz was about what had just happened.

"Not this early, sir." Lowering his voice, the officer said, "But it looks random. Like some crazy guy just went off."

"It's just that this trial already has been so eventful, so the idea of some crazy guy just going off seems awfully coincidental."

Nicki turned her head so that the police officer wouldn't see her smile as she watched Shep working him.

"One of the courthouse officers said he saw him trying other courtroom doors before finding this one unlocked."

"Ah!"

Shep was pleased with the information he had gotten so easily, and he didn't want to push it. He would want to go back and talk to that officer later.

"Well, if you two will follow me through the back, we have some vans waiting for courtroom personnel. We'll get you some coffee, or something, and get your statements so you can go on home."

"Thank you, officer," Nicki said. But she had no interest in going to the precinct to give a statement, and she wondered what happened to Rolex.

CHAPTER TWELVE

The next day news reports all around the country carried headlines that decried things like "Courtroom Massacre" or "Juror and 12 Others Gunned Down During Sensational Testimony." Reporters from other states began to converge on the nation's Capital and all the participants in the trial were afforded temporary protection while local and federal authorities tried to sort everything out.

By noon the next day, spokespersons for the local police and the FBI agreed that the juror who was killed was not the target of the gunman. None of the law enforcement agencies wanted rumors circulating that the shooting was a signal to the jurors about how the trial should come out. Of course, the timing of the shooting—right in the middle of Mr. Rolex's second testimony—was fodder for any number of conspiracy theories about Mr. Rolex's testimony and his real role in the case. Law enforcement officials buried him so deep in protection that even the prosecutor had trouble locating him.

Over the next few days Nicki grew furious that she had to deal with agents following her around, but there was so much going on with this trial, so many unanswered questions about the shooting, that she mostly just made bad jokes about agents following her into the ladies' room (and was otherwise disagreeable). But she dealt with it. And, of course, the trial was postponed indefinitely; it took days to process the crime scene—the third now in Nicki's world—and to clean up the courtroom.

Judge Sullivan wanted to set a new date for the trial to resume as soon as it was feasible. She did not want to give those who were responsible for the massacre in her courtroom the impression that they had made an impression—not on *her*!—and she did not want witnesses' memories to begin to fade or disappear altogether. Mostly though, she did not want to lose her own nerve to try this gruesome—and now even more complex—case.

CHAPTER THIRTEEN

"Hello?" Agent Stackhouse asked in a low voice.

The numbers on the clock looked blurry, but David was sure they said 3:42 a.m. After the U Street mess had begun to die down, someone in the White House had decided it would be good for the country, and the President, to change the subject altogether. Eleven countries in nine days; crowds in the tens of thousands. President Pierce was a rock star overseas. He had always been, so for the most part the Secret Service prepared for friendly venues. Anyway, it had been eleven days since David had gotten to sleep before two or three in the morning. He had just drifted off when the President called.

"Agent Stackhouse, President Pierce would like to speak with you," the White House Communications operator said.

"Yes, sir," Agent Stackhouse said, clearing his throat and sitting up in bed.

"David!" the President exclaimed as if it was a lot later in the morning, "Are you asleep?"

"Not anymore sir, no," David said dryly.

"Do you guys know anything about what happened downtown in court yesterday? Awful, isn't it?"

"Yes, sir. We're looking into it but right now it does not look like it was actually related to the case."

"Really? How's that?"

"Well, it's early. But the shooter was seen trying other courtroom doors before Judge Sullivan's," Agent Stackhouse said.

"Look a little bit harder," the President said, his voice lowering the way it did when what he was saying was urgent.

"Of course, sir."

There was a click, and the President was gone.

"Do you have to go?" Tommie asked turning over and snuggling David, her breasts pushing into his back. David liked it when she did that. He thought it was sexual without being overt and without expectation (though with the hint of anticipation).

"No," David said reaching back over his left side pulling her hand under his and against his chest.

"How long can you stay in bed?"

"Long enough," David said letting go of the seriousness in the voice he used when he was talking to the President.

"Mmmmm," Tommie whispered, snuggling him tighter.

"That's what I was thinking," David responded, leaving the sober matters he lived with day-to-day to lose himself in the giddy affairs of loving and distraction and peace. They didn't wake then; they both fell off to sleep for another hour or two, and when they woke, they had long, sleepy, slow sex until the alarm went off at 7:00 a.m.

CHAPTER FOURTEEN

Pass Christian, Mississippi, had two cab companies, a chemical plant where people worked until they retired, one nice restaurant and—since the late '80s—mammoth casinos where little old black ladies played the slots during the day, and cigar-smoking, scotch-drinking men and women played the blackjack tables all night. One of the town's two cab companies, American Pride, had a mere three cars, the other company just had one for hire. The night driver for American Pride only had one good eye. You could still see the bad eye in the socket, but it was sunken and squinty and didn't move when the other one did.

It was hard not to stare when you first got in Lenny's cab, but most riders, out of towners or drunken casino goers, thought staring was less awkward than blurting out "Eeeeeew! What happened to your eye?"

"This weather is unusual for us this time of year," the driver said to D.C. Police Chief Coley as he settled into the cab. "It's unusual for it to be this hot so early in the season. We don't usually get this kind of heat until July or August. Yup, this is very unusual weather for this time of year."

It almost sounded as if Lenny had gotten on a theme, on a loop, but did not remember he was on it, so he kept expressing the one thought that was in his head, over and over. When he did that, most of the passengers he had thought it was related to whatever happened to his eye.

"This is Main Street, correct?" Chief Coley said, hoping to see if he could get the broken record to skip to another groove.

"Yes sir, this is Main Street. If you follow it aaaawwllll the way down, it runs right into the beach," Lenny said.

"How far down is the beach?"

"About three more blocks," Lenny said. He pulled the cab over to the curb another fifty feet down and put the car in park. "Well, here you are, sir. The Sycamore House. I've never been inside it, but I'm told it's very nice. Might be the nicest thing in this here town."

"Looks nice," Chief Coley said reaching for a twenty-dollar bill. "How much do I owe you?"

"Seven-dollars and fiddy-eight cent," which was exactly what the meter said.

Anywhere else, Coley thought, he'd get charged extra for calling the cab, extra for the time the driver waited for him, extra for rush hour, etc. But this was small, sleepy Pass Christian, Mississippi.

"Keep the change," Chief Coley said, handing Lenny the crisp twenty. Coley never tipped that big unless he was paying for information, but it seemed appropriate.

The Sycamore House *was* a lovely restaurant—an old, historic house converted into an upscale restaurant. The original, though expanded, kitchen, the original maple staircase, and the pretty windows looking out over the wraparound porch made guests feel like they were being served in someone's home. That was the idea, the design, and Joe Peirinase was already sitting at the table in the farthest corner from the entrance when Coley arrived.

He looked different than Coley remembered him. He sat tall in his chair and for his fifty-seven years looked exceedingly fit, strong, and young. The skin on his arms was taut and the muscles in his forearms pushed his veins close to his skin like those in the arms of bodybuilders. His face belied his years as well. He had strong features but the skin on his face was still firm, not leathery looking like many men's skin at that age in a sunny climate. He didn't have any spots and his teeth were still fairly white, though that could as easily have come from a tube than Joe's genetics. The more Chief Coley looked at him, the less he was convinced he could be fifty-seven, no matter what supplements he might have been using.

"Joe," Coley said reaching out his hand, "thanks for meeting me."

"Pleasure. Happy to help. If I can. But as I said on the phone, I'm not sure that I can."

"What can I get you gentlemen to drink?" the waitress asked as Coley sat down. "Your usual, Joe?"

"Yes, ma'am," Joe replied. "A scotch-rocks, lime twist, and olives on the side."

"Same, without the olives," Coley mimicked. Joe looked puzzled at Coley's amusement.

"No harm meant," Coley said. "One of my old partners used to have the same order. Haven't seen or heard anybody have it since."

"What happened to him?"

"Killed."

"Joanne," Joe called after the waitress. "No olives."

"You don't have to do that on my account," Coley said.

"I'm doing it on my account," Joe said. "Precedent."

Lots of people in the Mississippi/Louisiana area were superstitious. Stories passed down from generation to generation about witchcraft and curses were more than urban legends there. Even if they weren't openly fearful or superstitious, most people in the area, particularly those living in the hills or woods, maintained a healthy respect for the old traditions. They simply did not do the things they thought could bring them harm or misfortune.

"Bad luck?" Coley inquired.

"Black magic," Joe responded. Coley sensed that Joe did not want to talk about whatever had spooked him, so he got them on task instead.

"Will we get into the plant tonight?"

"That's the plan," Joe said, "but it depends."

"On what?"

"On whether there are any incidents or incident reports tonight. If a processing or safety issue comes up, they lock down until they get it resolved and even Ernie can't get us in."

"How often do these incidents happen? What are our chances for tonight?"

"Pretty good. There hasn't been an incident in 387 days now. Some sort of record, apparently."

Just then Joanne came with the drinks and asked if she could take their order. Joe ordered a porter steak, bloody, and Coley ordered the catfish, offering a "when in Rome" explanation. The waitress smiled, took their menus back, and walked away from the table into the kitchen.

"So, how have you been, Joe? How's retired life?"

"Quiet, like I like it," Joe said, "until now," taking a friendly shot at Coley and his request.

"Well, back in Washington, we, well, *I* appreciate you taking the time to help us on this one. It's messy."

About six weeks after the U Street explosion, Coley had thought of the idea of bringing in outside help—help that wouldn't be tracked or traced. He had a tiny budget for things like that, and even fewer people he could trust with the idea so . . . there he was, himself.

"If I can," Joe affirmed.

Joe was always very, some felt exasperatingly, cautious. He regularly understated things—his capabilities, what he knew, what he could offer. Some people thought he was disingenuously self-deprecating, but Joe's father had taught—well, *beat* into him—that it was better to under-promise and over-deliver than the other way around. That way, you would never disappoint, he used to say. Joe's father had been a cop too, but he hadn't been in the military like Joe and there were lots of things Joe had seen in his life that separated his experiences from his father in ways that affected their closeness.

Joe and Coley chatted casually until the waitress came back with their food orders. Joe was already on his third drink by then but, Coley observed, neither his speech, wit, nor dexterity seemed to suffer. Coley had stopped halfway through the second round; he did not know what the night was going to bring, and he didn't want to have his judgment impaired even in the slightest, regardless of how well his colleague seemed to be holding his liquor.

"One more," Joe said holding up his drink, clanging the ice so the waitress could hear him. She had just left their dinner plates and walked away when he decided he needed just one more.

Coley thought, *I wonder what I am getting into, what Joe knows that I don't about what's going to happen tonight?*

"It's all right," Joe said to Coley reading the worry lines on his face. "I seem to be able to drink mightily in my old age, with no effect. A curse."

"What do you mean a curse?"

"You know, sometimes the dark side of life descends, and you just want to be numb for a while. Alcohol does that for most people but not me, and you know how I feel about drugs."

Joe had lost his first wife to a drug dealer he'd put away. The dealer was released from prison just five years into his sentence, but they were hard years, and he meted out his revenge upon Joe's wife, Chele. The dealer held her hostage in their house one night when Joe was on duty, holding off the SWAT team for thirty-five minutes until Joe could get there.

He had been on another call, and the dealer knew it. He'd been monitoring the police band. Then, just as Joe arrived on scene, the dealer walked Joe's wife outside the front door, stood her on the porch right under the porch light, stepped about twelve inches to the side, raised his Glock, and shot her point-blank in the side of the head.

Joe didn't even have a chance to negotiate with him. He would have given his own life for his wife's—he wouldn't have negotiated that for one minute. He would have just given his life, flat out. But he never had a chance.

The dealer was obliterated by the hail of bullets of all the other officers on scene—they had fired almost all their rounds into Chele's murderer, slicing him almost in half—but Joe never got over it, and later he had to be pulled from the undercover narcotics team altogether. Every single dealer after Chele's murder "resisted arrest"—at least that's what Joe put in his police reports to explain the condition they were in when they arrived at the precinct. In fact, Joe had been unable to control his rage and he beat the living hell out of every single one of them. One day the criminal court judge pulled Joe's captain aside and told him he knew Joe was beating the crap out of every dealer he handled because of his wife's death and that if the precinct didn't reassign him, the judge was going to dismiss all of the resisting arrest charges and set for trial all the defendants' claims of police brutality. That's how Joe ended up in the Special Operations unit and operated mostly out of D.C., where he stayed until he retired last year.

Joe and Coley lingered another hour over their dinners before Joe gave the nod to the waitress, paid the bill, kissed the waitress on the cheek, and left with Coley. It was only a ten-minute ride in Joe's car over Point Bridge to the plant. The plant sat on two hundred and twenty-six acres across Black Lake and was illuminated by tens of thousands of lights, lights that annoyed the Pass Christian residents, keeping them up at night. Neither man spoke during the short ride, each in his own thoughts. As Joe approached the first security gate, he dimmed his headlights, then put them on high beam, turned them off altogether, and waited. Seconds later, the gate opened, and he blinked his lights twice as he went through. He did the same thing at the second gate, although in reverse order, and proceeded to the third gate around the back.

"Get out," he said to Coley pulling up to the gate.

Coley started to ask, but then just got out. He stood there in the dark, by himself, for ten minutes before he heard the creak of a door opening. In the doorway was Joe, shining a small magnum flashlight under his chin so Coley could see who it was. Coley walked up the wrought iron staircase behind Joe, slipped inside the plant and followed Joe along what looked like a long corridor that ran underneath the main plant floor. Between the steel girders in the ceiling, Coley could just make out enormous vats and pipes and all kinds of machinery—machinery he'd never seen before—and endless rows of high-speed, high-capacity computers. Light peeked down through the grids periodically, and once or twice he thought he glimpsed the extension of a giant arm. Probably something robotic, like the kind you see at NASA working on the space shuttle.

When Coley checked his watch, it was 10:47 p.m., almost twenty minutes since they had arrived at the plant. It felt longer to Coley. Periodically, they would take a turn to the left or right, then walk what seemed like a hundred yards more. Six turns to the left, eight turns to the right he'd counted so far. The thin streams of light periodically sneaking through the girders had ended a while back. So did the steel grids, and the only thing that was lighted now was that tiny magnum flashlight Joe was holding.

Joe and Coley had not said more than a few words the whole time they had been walking. Now and then, Joe would say "to the left up here" or "to the right." Six times, left, eight times right. It occurred to Coley that he should ask how much further, but he didn't want to insult his old friend, or express distrust. Joe was doing the U Street investigation an enormous favor and until Coley had finally thought of and reached him, they'd pretty much run out of leads. They weren't sure whether the investigation was being deliberately stalled or whether they were just stuck. Coley had not heard from Agent Stackhouse anymore either. But when Coley talked to Joe, Joe seemed to have some ideas nobody else did.

Still, it was going on thirty minutes now, Coley thought.

Just as Coley started to say "Hey, Joe . . ." he smelled a horrible chemical-like, burning, fiery, smoky odor and within seconds, Joe was grabbing Coley's arm and yanking him down and into a side corridor, yelling at him to cover his mouth and eyes, and shoving some sort of mask in his face. It was not like any gas mask Coley had ever felt or seen. It covered his whole face and head, and it appeared to operate on its own. As soon as Coley touched it to his face, automatic arms, or sides, seemed to clasp and lock around something on the back, and a clear, flexi-glass mask flipped down from the top of his head, locked under his chin, and air started pumping inside the mask. Coley gasped at the first three or four breaths and it felt like his heart was stopping. For the briefest of moments, Coley wondered if he was being murdered. But then he got used to the air, which felt like the thin, cleaner air he experienced in Denver and South Africa.

For a while, the two men stayed crouched in the dark, breathing the thin air. Coley felt light-headed and weak, but his body was adjusting. Joe seemed to be fine, Coley thought, not having any trouble breathing. The strangest part, though, was that while it must have been a fire or some kind of explosion—maybe one of the "events" Joe had cautioned about earlier—Coley couldn't hear anything. Not fire crackling, or infrastructure collapsing, or wires sizzling, or fire-retardant systems going off—nothing. Maybe it was the mask. Maybe the explosion made him deaf. Maybe he *was* being murdered.

Just then, Joe motioned for him to get up and follow him. Obviously not deaf—or dead—Coley thought, relieved, and bemused at his own paranoia. And he followed Joe back the way they had come.

"When I do this," Joe yelled through his mask, grabbing a knob on the side of his own mask, "you do the same and haul ass, you hear me?" Joe yelled. "And I mean *haul ass!*"

"Yes," Coley nodded.

"Don't mess around, Jim!" Joe said, uncharacteristically using Coley's first name.

"Roger!"

Seconds later Joe flipped the release on his mask and took off; Coley flipped his mask and took off after him. Coley was surprised at how fast Joe could run, but he kept up with him and they kept running until they were all the way to the back door of the van that was idling at the bottom of the stairs at the back of the plant. Coley dived in after Joe, but it felt more like flying because someone had grabbed the front of his shirt and yanked him in. The van door was slammed shut by someone outside, Coley could not see who, and they took off through the first set of gates, then the second. Coley could hear the gates crashing down, but from behind them.

What the hell kind of van is this? What the hell is going on?

Minutes later they were back over Point Bridge, across Black River, looking out of windows that were not there before. Coley had not had time to adjust and was still sitting on his knees.

What he saw when he looked across the water dropped him from his knees to his haunches. Two hundred and twenty-six acres of chemical plant was gone. Leveled. There was nothing. Nothing but a weird colored smoke curling up through the stack towers.

Where are we? What on earth is going on?

Coley's phone rang. He felt all his pockets—he could not remember where it was. He had stopped checking his phone for messages earlier; it had not caught a signal for hours.

"Hello?"

"Coley? It's David. You all right?"

Coley did not respond. The phone just fell from his fingers as he passed flat out; Joe caught it.

"He's out, David, but he's fine," Joe said to Agent Stackhouse, picking up the phone.

"Okay, thanks, my friend."

CHAPTER FIFTEEN

Shook.

When Police Chief Coley woke up, he was back in his hotel room, in the dark, in Mississippi. He reached for his sidearm; it was still there, loaded. He got up and walked slowly around the room, gun drawn, peering into the bathroom, in the closet, out the windows, behind the curtains, under the bed. Nobody was there; nothing was disturbed, so he sank back down into an under stuffed chair, rubbing his temples. He had a terrible headache and the taste of copper in his mouth. He drank some water and turned on the TV. Every news station screamed "Breaking News" about the chemical plant explosion. Reporters donning gas masks between their stand-ups all conveyed the same thing: "Plant officials tell us they have no idea what happened. They appear to be shocked at the level of destruction of the plant."

You could see the EPA officials in the background of the shot walking around in full protective gear, carrying meters, taking readings, banging the sides of their meters, and shaking their heads. There was a good deal of speculation about why the readings were negative for some of the typical emissions with an explosion of that kind, and some of the news stations had scientists on their shows speculating that the emissions could be significant enough or of the type to interfere with the radio waves of the meters. One station reported that the telephone lines at the Environmental Protection Agency, the Department of Energy, *and* the White House were so jammed that the President couldn't get a call out which of course wasn't true.

The story reminded Coley of his cell phone; he remembered it ringing and being surprised since he had not gotten a signal since he'd been in Mississippi. He reached in his pocket; it was there, but there was no signal again. He used the land line to call his number, but it went straight to voicemail. He checked the battery; it was full, but he plugged the phone in an outlet anyway. Why did he remember hearing it ring at the plant?

Nothing in the news reports made sense either, he thought.

He was disoriented and frustrated, he had grime all over his clothes, and he was hungry. He ordered room service and headed to the bathroom for a shower. The shower felt nice. Coley liked long, hot showers, something his doctor warned him against; they dried out his skin and caused rashes. But they relaxed him and made him feel like he was getting a massage, so he took them that way anyway; he decided to worry about the cost another time. Maybe the hotel had some lotion.

He did not hear the knock at the door, or anyone calling his name, but when he came out of the bathroom Agent Stackhouse was sitting in that chair.

"David," Coley said nodding. He was trying his best to act like the silhouette he saw in the chair, before he could fully focus his eyes and make out who it was, hadn't just scared the living shit out of him.

"Coley," David said affectionately, chuckling. "You take the longest-ass showers I've ever seen."

"Man, it's good to see you," Coley said, doing that handshake/hug/pat on the back/all-in-one-thing that Black men do when they greet old friends. He was sure that if David was sitting in his hotel room, in Pass Christian, Mississippi, after everything that had happened, he was finally going to find out what the hell was going on. The chemical plant. U Street. Abby. Everything.

"Wanna put on some clothes, Chief?" David joked as Coley stood facing him in his towel. "Let's take a walk."

"Sure. Food coming, though."

"Yeah. Already sent it back," David said. "It looked like crap."

Coley laughed and headed back into the bathroom to get his clothes. It was the first time in weeks he felt like he was finally going to understand what was going on and how everything was connected. He was relieved David was sitting in his hotel room, waiting; he was happy that all this craziness could soon be over.

There are not a lot of decent places to eat in Pass Christian, Mississippi, most people opting for good ol' Southern homecooked meals. Besides the fancy restaurant in town—The Sycamore House— there was only one other, a place on the river: Johnny Be Good. It was a tiny walk-up shack where you could get fresh seafood cooked while you waited. When it arrived, you took your plate out back, sat on old milk crates, and ate it right there by the dock. Nothing fancy, but it had some of the best seafood on the entire Gulf. By the time David and Coley headed out, Coley's headache was gone, but he was ravenous. David suggested they grab something at Johnny Be Good's, and they headed to the water. They both picked out two-pound lobsters, grabbed some beers from the gas station two doors down, and staked out a spot on the crates farthest away from everyone else. There were plenty of people and the place was bustling as usual, despite the excitement and fright of the explosion. It took twenty or thirty minutes to cook the lobsters, so Coley ate oysters on the half shell with hot sauce and lemon and David ate mussels. Just as they were finishing their appetizers, the fake names they'd given the servers were called; they grabbed their lobsters, ate for a while, drank beer, and talked about nothing in particular. Nothing important. Movies, sports. More sports.

After a time, David said, "Let's take a walk."

The moon was shining on the water like someone had just turned the lights up. The waves, though gentle now, made the light dance in horizontal lines, disappearing when the tide went back out and reappearing when the tide returned. There was an eeriness, as if someone was darting in and out of shadows, hiding. But the air was warm and steamy, and Coley let the sound of the waves calm and relax him. He always did that when he was near the water.

Coley and David walked a while, much further than an after-dinner stroll would prescribe, and now they were off the dock, in the sand, right next to the water. Coley needed the feeling he got of being lost in space and time when he was near the water. The last couple of months had been some of the worst of his entire career. He was tired, frustrated, unhappy with the way the investigation was going, sick of being criticized for not solving such serious issues in his city, and exasperated with himself for being unable to put the pieces together.

Agent Stackhouse broke the comforting quiet in a hushed voice that, despite its softness, conveyed like a knife cutting through butter. Incongruous. Discrepant. Un-seeming.

"It was a genetic experiment. Government sponsored. We used the U Street location under the theory 'hiding in plain sight.' It did not involve humans. When it was on the verge of being discovered, we manipulated it to look like a crime scene from some cheesy horror movie. We needed time to do some other clean up, and we knew the findings would have investigators and reporters going for a while. I'm sorry I couldn't tell you sooner, Jim."

David paused here to let this sink in. Then added, because he couldn't hold it in any longer, "It had tentacles."

That's the biggest bullshit I've ever heard, Coley thought.

"Hiding it in the plant was easier, as chemical plants blow up from time to time."

"The plant," Coley echoed, still shell-shocked from Stackhouse's reveal.

"Sort of. The actual production of one of the bio-agents happened there. It was hidden pretty well from the public function of the company, but you can't take chances with these things."

"Chalk it up to my investigator's intuition, or skepticism, or the government's history of keeping terrible secrets, but this sounds too easy, David. I was at U Street. If you guys did all that shit on purpose, you're all crazier than I thought."

"It's an especially important, very confidential experiment that has broader implications than you can imagine. In America and around the world," David said. After a pregnant pause, "Even in space."

"Bullshit!"

David continued, "The idea that it could become known was—is—unthinkable. Worse than anything this government, or any government, for that matter, has ever done at any point at any time in history. Worse than Tuskegee, worse than Appalachia, worse than all the NASA missions gone wrong and why, worse than any plague, virus … " David paused here, ran a hand along the left side of his head, behind his ear, showing his confliction about it. "But also, maybe the best."

"That's a little bit dramatic, don't you think?"

"Coley, I know you think we can be sick-ass bastards sometimes, and we can, to be sure, but do you really think anyone who was not mentally disturbed could create a scene like that if it wasn't absolutely critical to do so? We didn't even come up with anything that sick. We used those crazy movie people in Hollywood to stage the scene." They walked in a tense silence. Coley was playing back David's words, looking for signals or clues to information he may not have given directly. He had a headache again, suddenly, and a weird ringing in his ear.

"Gotta get back," Stackhouse said. "Wanna ride? We can talk more on the way home."

"Sure," Coley said, hesitating. He was thinking through whether he was really finished down here in Mississippi; should he hang around and see what he could dig up himself? He trusted his friend, but this was all a lot. And what happened to Joe?

"Can we shoot by the hotel and grab my stuff?"

"We already got it," Agent Stackhouse said.

"What do you mean?"

"We got your stuff, checked you out, took care of the bill," Agent Stackhouse said hanging an arm around Coley's neck. "You know the brother is the Truth," Stackhouse laughed.

It reminded Coley of when they were younger, less encumbered by the seriousness of their respective jobs, and could hang out more often and more freely. Coley missed that. He wondered if David did, too.

"Man, I should have signed up for the Service when you did. You guys get all the perks, *and* all the girls," Coley said laughing.

"Yeah, we also get shot at," Agent Stackhouse said, laughing along with Coley.

"And what are cops, chopped liver? We get shot at more than you guys do. Plus, no one's really shooting at you; they're shooting at him, the President, the big guy. We're the real targets."

"Yeah, you're right, but you can duck! They pay us to throw ourselves in front of the bus."

"Okay, okay, you win," Coley said, "but you still get more perks," and they both laughed as they walked back down the beach.

Coley started to mention the headache and ear-ringing when a thunderous helicopter drowned out his words and landed several hundred yards in front of them on the beach. They hopped in and there was Coley's bag, briefcase, and an overcoat in a seat that had a card with his name on it.

"Man!" Coley said.

"You know I like to ride fly." David smiled.

After the short helicopter ride to one of Mississippi's air force bases, they hopped a small jet.

Coley's headache kept coming and going. He wanted more from Stackhouse. Stackhouse owed him more, he thought. He was holding up his end of the bargain, helping out, keeping secrets. But he was tired. His head hurt, his mind was foggy, and he allowed himself to drift off to sleep. Coley didn't wake up until the helicopter was landing at Joint Base Andrews where a cab was waiting to take him home. He noticed his phone had a signal now and saw a missed call from Joe. "I'll call you in a few days," David said to Coley, offering a hand. Was it an apology for the mess he'd dragged Coley into?

"Already sick of me and my questions?" Coley said, in a lame attempt to lighten the mood.

"Nah," David replied. "Just taking a couple days off."

"You? Taking time off? I don't believe it. No one will. Just adds to the mystique."

David chuckled and leaned in. "See ya later alligator," he said mimicking Abby.

Coley just shook his head, "So lame, David."

"Yeah, some mystique, huh?"

CHAPTER SIXTEEN

When Nicki's trial finally started again, another week had passed. But hardly anyone was sitting in the courtroom who was not directly involved in the case. Except for a tiny smattering of die-hard reporters, it looked like a different case from the one that had drawn packed crowds before the shooting. The increased security looked out of place with so few people in court, but Judge Sullivan wasn't taking any chances. She wanted to get through this case, get a decision from the jury, and move beyond all the questions. Twice now the case had gotten out of hand, and she did not want to get a reputation for being the kind of judge who, fault or no, could not control her own courtroom. Judge Sullivan wasn't having any of it.

When she brought the mallet down; it boomed in the empty courtroom. "Clerk, please re-call the case," Judge Sullivan said.

"The court will please come to order. Recalling the case of . . ."

Nicki was prepared for anything this time. She'd made a motion for dismissal and alternatively a separate trial—*who knows what's really going on here, but her client has already pretty much been exonerated*—but both motions were denied. In the days during the recess, Nicki had gone through every detail of the case again, over and over. She re-read every witness interview, re-checked every fact against her notes, and went over with Shep every tiny piece of evidence there was. She wasn't going to waste any time getting Mr. Rolex to put his testimony on the record, not after everything that had happened. She'd call him, get to the heart of the questions right away, and finish. Quick and dirty. In and out.

"Ms. Lewis, I assume you'll be continuing with Mr. Rolex?" the judge asked.

"Yes, ma'am."

"Bailiff, would you please get Mr. Rolex?" the judge directed more than asked.

She had also directed Mr. Rolex, again, to remain available, not to leave the city. After both local and federal law enforcement assured her that the shooting was a random act of a troubled man, she had no reason for concern about Mr. Rolex's appearance or re-appearance. The prosecutor had tried to keep Rolex from coming back with a motion that implied there was a safety concern, but Judge Sullivan had denied it the same day in a written order that admonished the prosecutor's office for trying to get another bite at the apple.

Peering over the top of her reading glasses, Judge Sullivan discreetly looked over the jury. They had been sequestered after the shooting, and her experience told her that sequestered juries were tired, impatient, restless jurors who, except for one or two whose personal circumstances are worse than being holed up in a mediocre motel room, couldn't wait to get home. Plus, they had watched one of their own get gunned down right in front of them. Judge Sullivan was looking for signs of weariness, frustration, outright hostility, even signs of fear. But the jurors looked fairly refreshed and calm. Better than they had looked after she had polled them individually for their suitability to continue to serve after the shooting. While she was confident in her decision to continue with the trial with these jurors, rather than grant the prosecution's motion for a mistrial, she couldn't imagine them getting through the entire ordeal unaffected, and if they were affected, how would that impact their jury service? But each juror had expressed commitment to continuing and completing their service. Some talked about how supportive their families were being. Others decided they had simply come too far along with the facts and testimony to let a whole new group of people decide, especially when they had invested so much time in understanding and evaluating.

Judge Sullivan was not sure whether the jurors were expressing civic responsibility, were just caught up in all the drama, or whether they all hoped to write books afterwards, but there was nothing in their responses that would justify starting the whole mess over. So, she had denied the prosecutor's request for a mistrial and had set the new date.

The news reporting on the trial were getting more sophisticated though, and some of the experienced reporters were starting to tie things together in a way that bothered her. The big question was, how could these seemingly inexplicable things that were happening really be unconnected? It was Washington, D.C. after all—the place where secret agencies did secret things, where cover-ups were common, at times—where presidents had stood in front of the public, in front of the world, and lied. Flat out. Judge Sullivan didn't want the sordid history of D.C. politics and punishment to impact the jury's judgment in what was clearly a terrible but local crime. She could only control what she could control, though, and she was doing that to the best of her judicial ability.

Most of the jurors were already looking at the doors at the back of the courtroom as they waited for the bailiff to bring in Mr. Rolex. Suddenly, their collective gasps echoed through the empty courtroom.

Nicki swung around in her chair; she blurted out "Shit!" Then, "Excuse me, Your Honor."

"Take the first seat you come to back there Mr. Rolex!" Judge Sullivan roared at the witness. "Just sit down!" she demanded. "Counsel! My chambers. Now!"

Again, it took several minutes for all the defendants' lawyers to get into chambers, and the jury was sent back to the jury room.

"I'm going to say this one time. I will *not* have more drama in this trial, in this courtroom! I will *not*! The disruption, surprise, crazy people shooting at us—it ends today, do you hear me? And somebody better tell me what the hell is going on or this thing ends right now."

Judge Sullivan was seething, angrier than Nicki had ever seen her. For her part, Nicki had gone back and forth about whether to ask for a mistrial herself after the shooting, or whether to join the prosecutor's motion. Some of the colleagues she had chatted with said it was a tough choice whether to go forward. Others thought she should get through it if she could because the evidence so far had really been helpful to her client. And who knows how the prosecutor might change his theory or approach the case the next time around? Nicki also had a good feeling about the jurors. She felt like she had developed a rapport with them and that they liked her even if they were not sure what to think of her client. So, she neither made a motion for mistrial nor joined the prosecutor's motion. But now Nicki just wasn't sure how much to fight with the judge over a possible mistrial. She had no idea how to respond to the judge's legitimate question. She had no idea why her witness showed up at court looking like that.

"Your Honor, I have been in contact with Mr. Rolex by telephone since the court's recess in this case. He never said a thing about being hurt in any way, he didn't sound like he'd been hurt, and he has been exceptionally anxious to get back to court and get this over with," Nicki offered.

"Mr. Prosecutor?" the judge shot at the government.

"Nothing Your Honor," AUSA Holden answered, shaking his head back and forth. "I have no information whatsoever."

None of the lawyers for the other defendants offered an explanation either.

"*Bailiff!*"

The bailiff was in her chambers in seconds, "Yes, ma'am."

"What the heck happened to that witness? Did he say anything to you?"

"Yes, ma'am. He said he was in a car accident. Got pretty banged up."

You could hear audible sighs of relief from everyone in chambers, including the judge. She let out a long breath.

"Well, I'll instruct the jury that Mr. Rolex has been in a car accident. Counsel, you need to get through your examinations as quickly as you can," the judge said to all the lawyers, and everyone returned to the courtroom.

Of course, everyone was wondering whether Mr. Rolex really had been beaten up, including the judge. Some speculated it was related to what he had, twice, not been able to get out from the witness stand. But Judge Sullivan had no intention of probing further on it. She was going to take her bailiff's word for it and that was that. But she worried it was not the whole story or worse, not a truthful story. AUSA Holden was still debating in his head whether to ask for a mistrial based on the appearance of the witness. Maybe he would garner too much sympathy. Maybe jurors would not believe he was in a car accident, and would inject dangerous speculation, innuendo into the deliberations. But after all the wrangling he'd done with the defendants' lawyers, he was the prosecution's witness, and the only good witness they had, so even if the case mistried, he'd have to use him again and who knows if he'd appear next time at all. Or disappear.

Plus, if he couldn't get a mistrial after someone shot up the courtroom and killed a juror, there was not much chance of getting one for someone who says he was in a car accident. So, the prosecutor kept his counsel, but he sat back in his seat unsure of whether he was making the right decision.

Maybe I should at least get an objection in the record, Holden thought.

"Mr. Rolex, will you be able to make it to the witness stand?"

"Oh yes, ma'am," Rolex said. He made a spectacle of pulling himself up from the seat by his crutches and hobbling up the aisle.

He had gotten pretty good with the crutches, easily maneuvering around the banisters and hauling himself up onto the witness stand. He looked a little less pathetic coming up the aisle because of how well he moved on those things and that made Judge Sullivan happier.

"You understand, Mr. Rolex, that you are still under oath?"

"Yes, ma'am."

"And we understand you have been in a terrible car accident, is that correct?"

"Yes, ma'am," Rolex answered after removing the apparatus that looked like it was holding his head on. "I'm okay, though. I'm here," he said, his voice trailing off as if he was making a much more profound statement than noting his geographical location.

"And the court greatly appreciates that, sir. Proceed, counsel," the judge said to Nicki.

"Mr. Rolex, geeeeez, I hate to even ask you anything. I feel like the breath from my words could make you hurt even more."

Nicki was being charming, of course, and reminding the jury after their recess from the case why they liked her before and why they should like her still. It worked. Some of the jurors chuckled a little and the tension that had been in the air let out a breath of its own.

"Do you remember where we left off before the recess, Mr. Rolex?" Nicki continued.

"Yes, ma'am. I was getting ready to answer your question about how I knew for a fact that your client was not involved in the beating death of poor Mrs. Campbell."

"That's correct," Nicki said nodding along as Mr. Rolex was answering. "Thank you."

"The truth is," Mr. Rolex continued, then paused for what seemed like forever.

"Mr. Rolex!?" the judge interrupted, "is there a problem?"

"No, ma'am."

"Then why aren't you continuing?"

"It's just that the last two times I got to this part, well, something has happened, and I didn't get to finish. I was waiting a little bit to give whatever awful thing that might happen again a chance to happen, or not." Rolex was being charming too and reminding the jury why they should still like him as well.

"Well, as you see Mr. Rolex, nothing has happened. So please continue," the judge said.

"Yes, ma'am. I will continue. My real name is Lawrence Tyler. It is not Anthony Barthomolu Rolex as I testified previously. I am truly sorry about that. It absolutely could not be helped." Rolex-turned-Tyler suddenly spoke with perfect English, diction, and ease. He looked exactly the same, but Rolex-turned-Tyler was a different man.

"I am an undercover officer with the D.C. Metropolitan Police Department. I have been investigating allegations that D.C. homicide detectives may have been engaging in illegal activities. By the time I got to the scene that night, there was nothing I could do but call it in. Your client," he said turning to Nicki, "Miss Gray . . . she ended up with Mrs. Campbell's ring because I gave it to her. I was hoping to get some information about the slaying."

The courtroom was dead silent.

"You motherfucka'!" Nicki's client, Miss Gray, was on her feet, halfway across defense counsel's table, shrieking at Detective Tyler. "You a damn' cop? You a goddamn cop?" The marshals rushed her and forced her back in her chair.

Judge Sullivan slammed the gavel down five or six times before order was returned to the courtroom. Nicki stood in the middle of the courtroom frozen as she analyzed everything she was hearing. *Act like you expected this,* a trick every young PDS lawyer learned. *Get yourself together. Ask your next question. Hurry.*

"Why did you wait until you were in court today to make your information known Mr. Tyler, is it?" Nicki asked using her training, anticipating the answer.

"The investigation is ongoing, Ms. Lewis," the witness answered, using Nicki's name warmly.

"Is?" Nicki asked, but she knew he was going to say that. She had counted on it.

"Yes, ma'am."

"Well, haven't you jeopardized the investigation with your testimony here today?" Nicki continued, uninterrupted. Everyone in the courtroom was absolutely glued to the witness stand, even the court reporter, and remained utterly silent. The prosecutor, who should have been on his feet screaming mistrial, demanding a meeting in chambers—something, anything—just sat there, stuck. He didn't know where the witness was headed but he did know Judge Sullivan looked even more angry than she had when she first saw Rolex-turned-Detective Tyler come in looking like the night of the living dead.

"My own duties in the investigation have been completed and uncompromised. The only thing in jeopardy, perhaps, is my own personal safety. But that goes with the territory, of course," he continued. "Let me state again for the record, though," he said, turning to Judge Sullivan, "I am terribly sorry this matter has been so difficult. I know that my part in it has not helped."

The judge did not respond but she appreciated Detective Tyler's words—she believed them, and that lowered her temperature. Suddenly, though, Nicki remembered. When they all started out as very young lawyers at PDS, they called him "LT" and the memory of that time, of Detective Tyler, who she was to him, almost made her pass out. Nicki searched her memory. She'd known an Officer Tyler. Years ago now, though. Could this detective be her officer? Could there be two LT's? *Nah*, Nicki thought, his face is all wrong.

Finally, AUSA Holden jumped to his feet. "Objection, objection, objection!" He said it so loud and with such force that it startled the jurors and caused the marshal up front to poise his hand on his sidearm.

"Counsel!" the judge scolded, "we heard you with the first 'objection.'"

"May we approach the bench, Your Honor?"

"Approach."

"Your Honor, I've never experienced anything like this in all the hundreds of cases I've prosecuted. It's outrageous and patently unfair to the state's position."

"What is this, the government's 'it's not fair objection?' I don't know that one," the judge retorted.

Man, she is in a bad mood today, Nicki thought. *I'm not saying jack!*

"My objection is notice, Your Honor, but may we please talk in your chambers?"

"Counsel, I really am in no mood for any more drama in this trial. Not one iota! Not even a little bit. What is it that we can't resolve at the bench?" the judge asked. There was a harshness to her own tone, so she softened it a bit.

"Your Honor, the government would like to better understand the circumstances here so that we can preserve whatever rights we have and make whatever appropriate objections on the record," AUSA Holden replied.

"Step back, counsel," the judge said. "Marshal, would you please escort Mr. Tyler back to chambers. Counsel, chambers. Members of jury, we will be taking a 30-minute recess. Do not speculate about this meeting or attribute any more or less weight to the witnesses' testimony because of this break. Do you understand?"

"Yes, Your Honor," the jurors responded, some nodding, some speaking.

"Does everyone understand?" the judge asked, looking at juror number seven.

"Yes, Your Honor," everyone responded, including juror number seven. Judge Sullivan had been watching juror number seven since they resumed the trial after the shooting. While the judge was more than satisfied this jury could and should continue the trial, and there was nothing in her polling of the members that concerned her, juror number seven was the only one of the twelve, plus two alternates, who was stoic during and after the shooting. He didn't look shocked; he showed no emotion at all. Rather, she thought, he was eerily collected and seemingly unfazed. He didn't even duck when the shooting started, the judge had noticed, as if he knew where the bullets were intended.

One of the jurors was killed randomly; how did he know he wouldn't get hit? the judge had wondered at the time.

So much was happening then that Judge Sullivan didn't revisit it in her mind or raise it in anyone else's. Not even Sam's, her bailiff, who never missed anything.

Maybe I will raise it with Sam later, she thought to herself now.

In chambers, Holden could hardly contain himself.

"I'm speechless, Your Honor," he began. I don't even know what to say. Nicki, are you telling me you really did not know anything about this? Not even a hint? Nothing?"

"What do you think—I want to get myself disbarred!" Nicki shot back. "I was as surprised as you were, and you know it. And even if I had a 'hint,' which I didn't, what the hell—sorry Your Honor—does a 'hint' require one to do? A 'hint' isn't disclosable, as you well know. Did you have one—a 'hint'? Did you mention it to anyone?"

"Of course, I didn't know anything about it—nothing!" They were shouting at each other now.

"All right, all right!" the judge interrupted. "I get it. You're shocked and chagrined, AUSA Holden, and you were caught unaware," she said to Nicki.

Nicki was angry but she wasn't worried, and she didn't mind the break in the action in the courtroom. The jurors needed time to digest what had just happened and try to piece things together. Plus, no matter what, her client was completely exculpated. Still, the old connection to LT stayed in the back of her mind.

He looks so different now. I wonder if he had cosmetic surgery after a dangerous case or something? Nicki thought.

"Does the government have an actual objection?" the judge said.

"Your Honor, after everything that's happened and how far we've gotten in the trial, I'm reluctant to ask for a mistrial again. But it feels like there is a fundamental—I don't know, um— fairness issue that could very well go to the ability of the jurors to make a fair and impartial decision. I need to work through the precise objection a little more, but I think you understand where I'm coming from and I think the bigness of this new issue deserves a longer recess so that the government can do that."

Holden obviously wasn't speechless, but he wasn't kidding when he said he didn't know what to say.

"For what it's worth, I don't have an objection to that, Your Honor," Nicki volunteered. The other defendants' lawyers did as well. They needed time to reassess as well.

"How many more witnesses do you have, Ms. Lewis?" the judge asked Nicki.

"Just two. Maybe one." She hadn't decided whether she now needed the second witness at all.

"Okay. We will take an early lunch today. You have two hours, counselor," the judge said to the prosecutor. Come up with whatever you're going to come up with or forget about it."

"Thank you, Your Honor" the prosecutor said and turned to leave chambers.

"Your Honor," Nicki said, nodding her respect as she left.

The judge called for her bailiff. "Would you ask Mr. Role—I mean Mr.—I mean Detective Tyler to come in. The back way."

"Yes, ma'am."

"Have a seat Detective Tyler," Judge Sullivan said to Tyler as he entered. "You've had quite a trial, haven't you?"

"Yes, ma'am. Again, I am sorry it has been such a disruptive trial, Your Honor. I assume you are all right?"

"Yes Detective, I'm fine." Judge Sullivan wondered if he would have asked that if she was a male judge.

"So . . . ," she continued. She wanted to learn a little more about what was going on, but there wasn't anything inherently wrong with his revelation—except the perjury part. She couldn't think of an appeals judge who wouldn't uphold the testimony under an extreme exception, given the circumstances. And who would prosecute him for it anyway, the government? *Of course not.*

"So . . . a little awkward, huh?" Detective Tyler interjected, sensing Judge Sullivan's hesitation. He knew she was struggling with wanting more information but not having a good reason to ask. His office's legal counsel had researched the question fully and made it clear that the law would support his actions under the circumstances, that there was virtually no likelihood of legal repercussions. Still, he wanted to help her.

"I'll share what little I can, Your Honor," he continued. "It won't be much, though."

"I appreciate your solicitousness, detective."

"The investigation has been on-going for more than two years. It involves very high-level ranks in the police department and other law enforcement agencies, and it is complicated. People have been killed. As you know."

"Well, I appreciate—" Someone knocked on the door.

"I'm sorry to interrupt, Your Honor," Marshal Waithe said poking his head just slightly in the door. "But you'll have to order lunch now if you're going to eat. The jury has already finished ordering."

"Thanks, Sam. I will be just a moment. Detective," she continued, turning back to Tyler, "I do not wish to put you in an even more awkward or dangerous position than you already are. I appreciate your time."

"My pleasure, Your Honor. And I assume you understand that my inability to share more has as much to do with your safety as it does mine, and with the integrity of the investigation." Detective Tyler rose and began walking toward the door.

"I do indeed, Detective," but the judge hadn't actually thought of that until the moment the detective had said it. It also just occurred to her that the detective had not told her anything that he hadn't already said from the witness stand.

Judge Sullivan ordered her usual sandwich and chips and asked Sam if he would join her in her chambers for lunch.

"Sam, do you think the jury has been doing okay since we've been back in session?"

Sam knew the judge was really just referring to juror number seven—he had noticed him too and had been keeping a watchful eye.

"He's definitely a hard one to read. He is completely calm and unaffected through all that has happened. But, coming from his Gulf War service, perhaps there just isn't a lot now that would startle or frighten him. I have to say, he is an interesting subject and I have been keeping an eye on him. Something about him," Sam's voice trailed off a little.

"Well, let me know if you notice anything particularly peculiar," the judge said, more as a statement than a request. "Have you noticed his interaction with the other jurors at all?"

"That's the thing. He is 'Mr. Personality' around the other jurors privately. They all seem to like him. I will be surprised if he's not nominated jury foreman."

That worried Judge Sullivan even more. It was almost as if juror number seven was being deliberately poker-faced in the courtroom and the complete opposite outside it.

Was he trying to influence the verdict already? No real way to know at this point.

"Well, let me know," she said to Sam.

"Of course, Your Honor. Are you going to finish your chips?"

"Be my guest. You didn't eat your sandwich."

"No, ma'am. I will later. For now, I'll just finish your chips, if you really don't mind."

Nicki and Shep were eating their sandwiches on the same bench they always did when they needed privacy. It was cold out, but Shep had some information about all that had been going on in the trial.

"Man, are they locked down on this. I don't think I've ever seen the details of an investigation locked down so tightly. There're always leaks, always someone who's willing to say something. Man!"

"Oh, that's helpful," Nicki said. She knew he had something. He always did.

"Well, it really is a big deal, one of the biggest internal investigations in history, apparently. It goes all the way to the top and across several different law enforcement agencies which is why there has been unusually high cross-agency cooperation. It's set up so no single agency knows for sure which is the lead agency so everybody's walking around on eggshells and bending over and trying not to step on people's toes. Your guy, LT, do you remember him?" Nicki was hoping not to get into it with Shep but at least it was Shep.

"They had to change his face."

"What do you mean?"

"What do you mean, 'what do I mean?' That's LT."

Nicki looked down, shook her head.

"That's what I thought, but I wasn't sure."

The idea that she could have had a lover she would later fail to recognize was freaking her out.

"He's been in some shit, I have to say," Shep continued. "And he's been all over. He spent a couple years in Syria, a year in—"

"Syria! What the hell was he doing in Syria? Is he a spy?"

Nicki could hardly believe what she was hearing but then again, she could.

"Well, that would explain why we fell out of touch," she said facetiously, looking off across the park.

"What?"

"Nothin'. Just, well . . . nothing."

Nicki decided against sharing the sordid details.

"Anyway," Shep continued, noting what Nicki said, but also her demeanor.

"This incident, your incident—or murder, was just an extraordinarily unfortunate accident of space and time, and poor Mrs. Campbell ended up the poster child for the worst 'wrong place, wrong time' ever."

"Shep, what the hell are you talking about? Mrs. Campbell basically had her guts ripped out through her ass! How on earth is that just wrong place, wrong time? Getting shot, maybe. Getting stabbed, maybe. But not that, Shep. It doesn't make sense."

"It's horrendous. No question about it. But my info is good," Shep said.

"Here's the deal. The investigation Detective Tyler referred to involved four law enforcement agencies, a civilian contractor, a top-secret government-contracted lab, some very wealthy individuals, a couple of foreign interests, and maybe the Supreme Court—but that's been harder to pin down. And the White House."

"The White House? The White House, White House, or the *White House*?"

"The White House. Not the President. But some people around him. And his illegitimate daughter," Shep responded.

"The *President* has an *illegitimate* daughter? Yeah, right, and I guess she's Black too, huh?"

"Well, as a matter of fact—"

"I don't believe it. It's too much, Shep. Too much like a goddamn movie. I do not believe any of it. I think your sources are playin' you this time, dude!"

"Some of that is why more of it hasn't leaked, or at least gotten around law enforcement circles. It *is* too crazy to believe so the limited people who hear it do not believe it. Interesting strategy if it was intentional."

"All right, so . . . what does any of this, if it's true, have to do with Mrs. Campbell? No matter how big it is, it can't have been ok for anyone to abuse her like that to cover up something."

"You're right, of course. Mrs. Campbell was taking a short cut through the alley. As best people can figure out, there was some sort of exchange going on, exchange of information probably. They were using a courier—a thug—who only had to carry coded information. But in trying to be too clever by half, they chose poorly. He was a real thug, and he brought his boys along, and when they saw Mrs. Campbell cutting through the alley, they mistook her for a lady who had testified against one of their boys in court. He got sent up for life, no parole, and they went after her. They were trying to send a message to the other witnesses in a related trial. But they had the wrong person. They just had the wrong person," Shep said, shaking his head.

"Fuck!" Nicki said. "*Fuck*. I mean, this grandmother, still working because her deadbeat sons-in-law left their wives and kids with nothing, and she's just trying to keep them off welfare. Working, cooking for all those kids, trying to teach them right from wrong; alone because she won't re-marry after her one true love dies. I don't understand it."

Nicki was now on a rambling, emotional trajectory.

"It's cliché but why do such awful things happen to people who are just here, struggling, trying to make it, trying to help people who by rights should be helping them? I bet Mrs. Campbell didn't do anything bad to anyone her whole life, not one thing! I bet she didn't even raise her voice to her kids or her grandkids, and worked hard, and didn't complain, and saved her money, and didn't indulge when she could have, and was faithful to her husband of 30 years even though he probably wasn't and—"

"Come on, Nicki. In a minute she's going to be eligible for sainthood."

Shep wanted to keep the increasingly manic litany from plunging into hysteria and Nicki laughed a little, finally lightening up. She needed to vent, Shep knew that. She was venting not just about the new information but about the case in general. While she believed her client was innocent, the idea of being on the defending side of such a brutal, brutal murder had been keeping her up at night since the arraignment. That had almost never happened in all the time she'd been in the PD's office. It did not help that her client was such a thug herself; she had acted arrogant, cavalier, and basically insufferable ever since her arrest. Their first meeting was an argument, with Miss Gray disparaging public defenders even though she had no money for her own counsel. She insisted that Nicki call her 'Miss' Gray and bet her lock-up mates that her "court-appointed lawyer" would not be able to get her out. Nicki had almost walked away on the spot. But she had taken a deep breath and had that come-to-Jesus discussion with her new client.

"Okay, so where does LT come in?" Nicki said to Shep.

"Apparently, LT has become the go-to-guy for some of the stickiest shit on the planet. He has been working double undercover, maybe triple—most people put few things past his abilities, and some people even think he's in charge of the investigation but that would mean he's really a Secret Service agent posing as an undercover police officer, which no one thinks he is.

"Anyway, he was supposed to be the contact information exchange conduit but when Mrs. Campbell happened through, well, you know ... the whole thing went to shit," Shep continued. "No pun intended. It is still on-going, but the portion that has to do with the trial is basically over, like LT said.

"What's the deal with you two anyway?"

"Who?"

"Come on."

We have known each other way too long and hard for you to bullshit me now, Shep thought.

Nicki knew she was not going to get away with trying to be coy with Shep. She was just buying time before the inevitable reckoning.

"All right, all right, all right," Nicki labored. "It was a long time ago. Almost fifteen years. We were both just babes in the woods. He was a young officer; I was a young public defender. We thought the police were the devil back then, you know. There was no fraternizing, intermingling between the police and PDSers. It just wasn't done, at least not openly.

And I was one of the most die-hard of the group. You may not remember that about me," she said laughing, and they both cracked up.

Shep was no stranger to the level of Nicki's commitment as a defender and they had had plenty of funny and tough moments to prove it. It had been a big joke between them for many, many years.

"Anyway, we hung out pretty tough for a little over two years, sort of secretly. A couple of people knew. My closest, closest friend. His brother and a buddy on the force in L.A. Then he was promoted and doing felonies and then felony murders and then became detective, so it was just too hard to keep up the charade. Then, the next thing I knew he was gone—no one seemed to know where he was, though there was all sorts of talk about it. Remember? Some people said he was on the take and had to go underground. I knew that wasn't true. Some people said he had too much integrity for that and was probably deep undercover."

"What did you say?" Shep asked. "People must have asked you?"

"Yeah," Nicki said, her voice trailing off again. "Yup!" she added quickly, more upbeat, as if snapping back to the present. "I said of all the sleazy cops I knew, he was the least sleazy and I didn't think he was doing anything improper but that he was probably doing something undercover that would eventually screw up one of our clients so what the hell, let him stay undercover as long as possible."

Shep had picked up a little more than he had shared with Nicki about LT's life but this seemed as good a place as any to conclude the conversation—on more of a high note than a low one. It was going to be time to return to court soon. They finished eating and threw their trash in the mesh trash bin near the old oak tree that lawyers and clients sometimes use as a landmark when they are meeting up before court.

CHAPTER SEVENTEEN

We were together. I forget the rest.
—UNKNOWN

It was cold at the lake this time of year, but it was pretty. Quiet. Still. You could hear the striper fish splashing right under the surface, their fins making tiny ripples that turn the surface into tiny blinking Christmas lights.

Only a few people knew David owned a cabin on Lake Anna in Virginia. Even though it was located just ninety minutes from D.C., it was still unpopulated by the Washington set. David's cabin was right on the lake—too close, some people said, four and one-third acres, and away from the new subdivisions that were being built nearby. The cabin was surrounded by dense, tall trees that hid the moon at night. There was a one-lane private road going in and out, a three-car garage, a basketball court, outdoor sauna, and a wall of windows that looped around from the back of the house to the side, offering breathtaking views of the water. The house had its own private dock and a thirty-foot speedboat swayed in the slip. Even fewer people knew about the speedboat David had bought through a third-party at a government auction of confiscated items. It was all perfectly legal, but he had not wanted the sale traced back to him.

David kept a bicycle at the lake, too. When times were particularly stressful, he rode until his legs were too fatigued to pedal one more foot. Inevitably, a kind and respectful neighbor would see him walking his bike and give him a lift to the top of his road. That's the way the locals knew him—as David, the guy who rode so hard his legs ached too much to get him home, the guy who needed a lift from time to time. He thought that was funny, given what his day job was.

He kept a bike there for Tommie as well, and an air hockey and ping-pong table—they brought out the fierce competitiveness in her. He thought that was funny too.

"Feel like spaghetti?" Tommie called to David from the kitchen. "It's too cold to barbeque, don't you think?"

"Spaghetti's good. I say pasghetti, you say pasghetto, pasghetti, pasghetto, pasghetti, pasghetto, that's what it's all about." David sang the words to the old movie classic theme.

Things had quieted down, for now, but the President was going to change all of that shortly, and for a long time. He needed to enjoy his time with Tommie, however brief.

"Silly man."

David walked across the dining room into the kitchen and scooped Tommie up in his arms.

"I'm going to feel that tomorrow," he laughed, carrying her to the bedroom and laying her down gently on the bed.

"You're not hungry anymore?" Tommie asked.

"Yeah, I'm hungry," David said softly, pulling Tommie on top of him.

It seemed like only minutes had passed when David's cell phone danced across the nightstand, vibrating fiercely. The evening had turned into early morning.

Seconds later, Tommie's phone skidded off her side of the bed and fell on the floor.

"I have to go, baby," David said, swinging his legs over the side of the bed. He got up with both his hands on his lower back.

"Me, too," Tommie said. "And, your back hurting is not from carrying me fifteen feet to the bed, you know."

"Yeah, then what *is* it from?" he teased.

"You know what I'm talking about," she called back from the bathroom. "If you weren't so, so . . . animated last night, you might not have a sore back at all!"

Tommie turned the shower on and the playfulness off and hurried to dress.

"See you later, baby," David said, peeking around the bathroom door into the bathroom.

"Okay. Have a good day."

"You, too. Call me later."

Tommie finished her makeup and pulled on clean clothes she kept at the cabin. She hurried to her car and sped up the highway getting briefed and brought up to speed by cell phone almost the whole way.

It's true what they say about cell phones and driving, even hands-free, Tommie thought as she waited at the South Gate to get cleared into the White House. *I do not remember that ride at all,* and she promised herself she would not keep doing that, no matter how urgent the circumstance. Plus, she was still late.

"Hi, Julia," Tommie said, "how are you? Everyone already in there?"

"Yes, but they're just getting their coffee and haven't started so you're OK," Julia said smiling at Tommie. "Plus, you know you're one of his favorite chiefs, but don't tell anyone I said that—all the other chiefs of staff will get their feelings hurt."

Julia liked Tommie. She always went out of her way to be respectful to staff and if you did not know she had such an important job you wouldn't have guessed it from how she treated them. That was not true of a lot of the other senior executives in the Administration and for the life of her, Tommie could never make that work in her head.

"Wish me luck," Tommie said to Julia, winking at her as she walked through the door to the Oval Office Julia held open for her.

"You'll be fine, as always," Julia whispered back as Tommie passed her by. "You look nice, by the way," Julia said, helping Tommie relax a little.

"Come on in, Tommie," the President said as she walked in. "Have a seat. We're just getting coffee. We roused you awfully early this morning, didn't we?"

"No problem at all Mr. President, of course."

"Your boss, Homeland Security Secretary Brown, is running a bit late. We have him on a secure line until he gets here," the President said to everyone in the Oval Office.

"Good morning, Mr. Secretary," Tommie said to the speakerphone on the table.

"Mornin' Thomasina, you all right?" the speaker phone said back.

"Yes, sir, fine sir. You?"

"Fine, fine."

"And you know Agent Stackhouse of course, Tommie?" the President said to Tommie.

"Y-y-yes, sir, of course, sir," Tommie said stuttering just enough to get attention but not enough to rouse suspicion. At least that's what she hoped. "Agent Stackhouse," Tommie said nodding at David.

"Ms. Coles," David nodded back.

He was much better at this than Tommie was; fortunately for the two of them they had not had to practice it much. Even though the U.S. Secret Service was technically housed in the U.S. Department of Homeland Security, David's office was in the Old Executive Office Building right across from the White House, as was a lot of the President's Protective Division, until they got their fancy new building on H Street. So, while technically the Secret Service was one of Tommie's responsibilities as chief of staff at the U.S. Department of Homeland Security, she had been able to avoid circumstances where she had to weigh in on something that had a direct impact on David or his office. It was only a matter of time though, they both knew, and their relationship was clearly against the rules in any event.

They had not intended it. They were just around each other a lot in their respective roles and they grew to respect, then admire, then care for, then love each other. They happened upon their feelings backstage at an economic event where the President and the Homeland Security Secretary were speaking one day. They'd spent months at first—almost a year, keeping a professional distance. But their feelings persisted. So, it began, haltingly, with trepidation, anxiety, and disquiet. Tommie hoped the burden of it would be too much and it would collapse of its own weight. David thought his near daily travel with the President would make it easier for both of them—an out-of-sight out-of-mind kind of thing. But theirs was more of an absence-makes-the-heart-grow-fonder kind of thing, and while their professional experiences were completely different, their respective positions afforded them an awful lot of commonality.

"Shall we get started?" President Pierce said, sitting down on the navy couch next to the end table.

He always sat in that corner of that couch. First-timers to the Oval Office were instructed so before they entered. One time though, a visitor missed the instruction and collapsed into the President's spot. He had already sunk deeply into the couch before he noticed the "man, what were you *thinking*?" stares from the President's staff. He jumped up with apologies, but the President had graciously invited him to stay where he was.

"Sorry," the President had told him, "my staff acts like that spot on the couch is the only place my butt can find to park itself but, you know, in my experience, butts will sit just about anywhere you lower them."

Everyone had laughed, which was the President's point. It just was not that serious of a thing.

"All right, let's get going," President Pierce said. "Who's first today?"

"Mr. President, if I may?" the speakerphone asked.

"Certainly, Bob, go ahead."

"Mr. President, as you know, we have been working with a number of agencies in investigating whether the F Street murder trial, the U Street fire, and the Pass Christian explosion are connected, whether they are part of a larger terrorist plot to divert multiple investigative agencies from counter-terrorism efforts. We wanted to report on the progress of all of that and raise some other issues with you."

Tommie looked at Agent Stackhouse who was pretending to look at notes. She thought she saw him exchange a glance with the President.

"Yes, go on," the President said.

"To date we have been unable to find a nexus but there has been an interesting development at the trial. The key witness known as Anthony Rolex, who appeared to be a thug, is really an undercover officer who was investigating a high-level corruption matter—or worse—and was on duty at the time of Mrs. Campbell's brutal murder. We have not gotten very much on the investigation yet, but it is rumored to involve people at some of the highest levels in a number of agencies and . . . " Homeland Security Secretary Robert Brown said, pausing—he did not want to say the next words out loud—"the White House."

"Let me say," he continued, "we have no reason at this point to believe there is any undisclosed investigation going on related to the White House, but it is a fairly strong rumor so we're calling in a number of chits to find out what's going on."

Secretary Brown did not want to have this part of the conversation on the phone when he could not see the President's face or access his body language in hearing this news. But when the President is ready to start a meeting, you start the meeting. There was no reaction. Not one of shock or even surprise. There was barely even perceptible curiosity. Tommie noticed it too, David could tell from the glance at him she failed to catch before it left her thoughts and shot across the coffee table.

"Mr. President," Secretary Brown continued, "there *is* a matter we need to discuss in this regard—"

"I'm sorry to interrupt," Julia said, "Mr. President, but Prime Minister Claire is on the line for you."

"Apologies, Bob." The President nodded to Julia and then to Tommie and the rest of the staff in the Oval Office. "Gentlemen, Tommie," the President said, "please give me a moment."

With that everyone stepped into the tiny reception area and chatted with Julia while President Pierce talked with the British Prime Minister. Homeland Security Secretary Brown was at the West Gate by then, so he just dropped off the call and made his way to the West Wing.

"How're the grandkids?" Tommie asked Julia.

"Wild, as usual. I do not know how I ended up 'granny' to such wild, unruly children. In my day . . . " she trailed off, as everyone laughed.

Julia often lamented that her son's kids were being raised too leniently, too freely, and with too many privileges. She wasn't old fashioned, really, but she worried that her son and daughter-in-law, like many parents today, she said, were too concerned with being liked by their children to impose important discipline. Of course, she spoiled them rotten like any good granny, but the parents were supposed to take up the slack she believed, and she could not see how they could grow up and be independent and take care of themselves if they only learned the luxury of privilege and comfort, and not the lessons of hard work and sacrifice.

"Well, they're entirely proper and well-behaved when they visit the White House I am told," Secretary Brown said as he came through the door.

"Mr. Secretary," Julia said. "Nice to see you in the flesh. You move around so much, I was beginning to think you were just a disembodied voice." The gathered staff collectively chuckled.

"Is he still on?" Secretary Brown asked nodding toward the door to the President's office.

"No, but he's not quite ready. I think it will be just a sec, though." At that moment Julia's intercom buzzed.

"Yes, Mr. President?"

"You can send them back in."

"Yes, sir," Julia said to the group nodding her head toward the door.

"Mr. President," Secretary Brown said extending his hand.

"Bob," the President said, greeting the Homeland Security Secretary. "Go ahead."

"Thank you, Mr. President. I did want to check in on that other matter."

"Sure, Bob. Let's have Julia set something up separately."

"Yes, sir."

"Anything else?"

The President scanned the room, being careful to give each glance the same amount of time.

"No, sir."

"No, thank you sir," the others repeated.

"Tommie?"

"Mr. President," Tommie began warily. "Since a number of us in this room have just heard the preceding exchange, it might be prudent for White House counsel to provide a written document that could be used should any of this issue turn out badly and becomes public."

Tommie's position as chief of staff to a cabinet secretary meant it was her job to protect her secretary and the President the best she could, to watch their backs, and to implement their policies and plans. She liked the watching-their-backs part of the job better than any other—it was more natural to her than her other responsibilities, and she was good at it. The messier a situation was, the better she liked it, and the higher she rose to the challenge of fixing it. Being the behind-the-scenes-person suited her fine. The people who counted knew what she did and that was enough for her.

"Smart, as usual," the President said turning to the Secretary. "Bob, if you didn't already have her ... well, don't hold it against me if she ends up over here before it's all said and done."

President Pierce was careful to say that playfully. He did not want his good cabinet secretaries to worry that the White House was going to raid them and steal their good people, though they did it all the time. But he had known for some time that eventually Tommie would end up in the White House, possibly as Staff Secretary or maybe even White House Deputy Chief of Staff.

Tommie blushed out loud with a small, uneasy laugh.

The Secretary joked, "You'll have to beat me at one-on-one, Mr. President, and we all know you can't hit the side of a barn with an M1 Abrams tank."

"I wouldn't be so sure, Bob—I've been practicing. Didn't you see the hoop I had put up out back?"

"No, sir," Secretary Brown laughed, "but I suspect you have little time to practice, and my skills are formidable."

"All right, all right," Julia interrupted, slipping into the Oval Office without notice, except for Agent Stackhouse, who noticed everything. "Game's over, gentlemen, and lady, the President has people waiting."

Julia usually knew exactly when to come into the Oval Office, and in all the years she worked for President Pierce, she had never made a mistake, never misjudged the situation. President Pierce used to wonder if she kept her eye to the peep hole the whole time he was in a meeting, but he knew better since she was also answering the phone and receiving visitors and taking care of packages and items dropped off for him. He didn't know how she did it all, and when he would ask her, she would just tease him, rather uncharacteristically, saying that "a girl has to be able to keep some things to herself."

Everyone began to gather their belongings and file out, Agent Stackhouse trailing behind, as always. As Tommie was walking out into the waiting area outside the Oval Office, Stackhouse started behind her, but President Pierce called after them both.

"Agent Stackhouse, Tommie, a moment?"

Just then Tommie turned around as if she was in slow motion, trying too hard not to show her surprise or dismay.

Now back in the Oval Office, behind closed doors, President Pierce said, "You guys would make a cute couple, you know, if it wasn't against every rule there is."

With that he winked and walked toward the bathroom.

"Mr. President!" David called after him, objecting to the characterization. "I believe you've embarrassed Ms. Coles."

"But not you, I would guess," the President said, closing the bathroom door behind him.

Tommie shot a strained look at David before hurrying out of the room as to not raise any more suspicion. She rushed to catch up with Secretary Brown—a perfect escape she thought, having to ride back with the Secretary to the Homeland building. As she settled in the car, her cell phone rang.

"You OK?"

"The Secretary appreciates your help on this," Tommie answered non-responsively.

"Oh. Are you in the car with him?"

"Yes, very much," Tommie responded.

"See you later, then?"

"Why don't we touch base in the morning after you have more information?" Tommie was shaken by the President's remarks. Surely, he was not aware of her relationship with the head of his protective detail. But President Pierce was never random—not in words or deeds. He was always deliberate and intentional, even in jest.

Well, nothing to be done about it this second anyway, she thought.

"All right," David said, his voice dropping like a stone from disappointment and concern. "We'll circle back tomorrow."

David worried that with the way things still were in the world, Tommie would bear the brunt of the situation if it were discovered. She would almost definitely have to resign, and while the political folks would likely try to ensure she had a soft landing, the situation would almost certainly damage her reputation. As a man, protecting the President—the relationship he had with the big guy—he would barely be touched by a scandal like that. He would step aside, likely, for a short time while there was an internal agency investigation into whether there were any occasions when his judgment or ability might have been impaired because of the relationship. But everyone knows how that would turn out—just fine. Mostly, though, he worried constantly that Tommie would get spooked by the whole thing and end it, and he just didn't know what he would do if she left him. He loved her. More than he had ever expressed to her, he knew. He would kill for her, he knew. Without blinking. Without a second thought.

CHAPTER EIGHTEEN

Some of the press had begun to move on to other stories after Fire Chief Ramsey and Chief of Police Coley shut down the information flow on the U Street fire (and the F Street murder case was almost over). Nicki's last two defense witnesses went on and off the stand without incident. They made the points Nicki needed them to make, their credibility was not impeached by the prosecutor, and most importantly, there were no surprises. So, Nicki rested her case. The prosecutor requested and was granted a short in-court recess to whisper with his team about whether they should put on any rebuttal witnesses. Their case didn't stink to high heaven but a bunch of it had turned to garbage and AUSA Holden knew there was nothing to do now but stand the can up and close the lid on it.

"Closings tomorrow morning at 9:30," the judge said. "Court adjourned."

But there were a couple of veteran reporters whose instincts told them there was "there, there." The experienced reporters believed something covert was happening and they wondered how high up it went and who would eventually lose their jobs over it. The law enforcement officials involved in the cases also knew those veteran reporters would stick with the story no matter what they told them—that is why they had worked so hard to cut off access and information. Unanswered questions, unresolved issues, they knew—it was blood in the water to them, and they would not stop circling until something was devoured.

It was beautiful the morning Nicki was getting ready to do her closing. But, unlike every other closing she had done, she actually lost sleep over this one. She wrote it and re-wrote it. She practiced it, then she did not want to practice it. Stoli, Nicki's cat, heard it over and over. For the first time in her career Nicki felt like if she did a good job and got her client off, she would go to hell. Or maybe just bad stuff would happen to her from now on.

These sorts of insecurities did not fit into the life she deliberately lived. Nicki believed that everyone was entitled to a good defense and that the indigent were screwed by the judicial system. Plus, she hated losing, maybe more than she loved winning, so any angst that could result in her actually blowing a closing—or worse, purposely blowing a closing—was inconsistent not just with what she believed, but with who she fundamentally was as a human being. Nicki defined herself, as much as others had defined her, as a world class trial lawyer. She was terrible at compromise or negotiation and she was most at home in front of a jury. She was scary-smart on the law and the good judges appreciated her intellect. So, none of it made sense. Not all the drafts, not all the mock arguments, and certainly not her indecision about her closing argument outfit. Generally, Nicki "didn't give a flying fuck... whatever that means" about things that she wore as long they were professional and smart. But today, this day, she could not even decide what to wear.

"Is counsel ready to proceed?" the judge asked.

The courtroom was packed for the closings. The judge refused to allow cameras in the courtroom, as many of the younger judges were doing, so the rows were packed with reporters and families and other lawyers. After half an hour of back-and-forth, Nicki had finally decided on a simple but stylish blue suit, a white cotton shirt, two buttons open.

She looked good. Nicki had always thought that the women lawyers who buttoned their shirts all the way up to their collar, while looking professional, also gave the jury the impression that they were stuffy—not like regular people—and she thought the jury couldn't tell what their real personalities were like. She believed that jurors liked to know, or at least speculate, about the lawyers in a case, particularly the defense lawyers. Plus, if you were not buttoned to the neck, you could be a little easier with yourself, something she thought was particularly important in a nasty case like this.

When it was her turn, Nicki began with the professionalism, ease, and comfort her clothes afforded, "Ladies and Gentlemen of the jury, I worked all night on my closing, literally. Really, you work on them all during a trial, but then a day or so before the case rests, you have to re-work and re-work and re-work it until it's right. Actually, a lot of lawyers do a first draft after the first day. It helps you stay organized and gets down on paper the ideas you had before the trial came along and screwed everything up."

"Counsel is there a point to this Trial Practice 101 lesson?" the judge interrupted.

"Yes, Your Honor. I'm getting right to that."

"It was really good," Nicki continued. "No, really, it was one of the best closing arguments I ever wrote." She was loosening the jury up, hoping to get them to laugh.

"You would have been dazzled," she said continuing to get mileage out of the jury's willingness to be led down this path. "But after hearing the prosecutor's closing—and you'll hear from him one more time because, since he has the very high burden to prove my client is guilty, he gets the last word. Still, even knowing I won't have a chance to talk to you anymore after that, I have decided not to waste any more of your time. However stupendous my argument was." It worked. Many of the jurors laughed. Others smiled.

Nicki continued to milk it. "Because in the end," she offered almost as a question, "at the end of the day, only two things I could say matter. I could pace back and forth in front of you like I usually do, probably making some of you feel like yelling 'sit the hell down, or at least stand still!' But in the end, after it's all said and done, only two words matter. So, I'm just going to say those two words."

And with that, Nicki turned, stuffed her hands in the side pockets of her skirt and walked slowly toward the defense table. Her client, along with everyone else in the courtroom, stared in anticipatory silence, their eyes following her every step. When Nicki got to counsel table, she turned back around and leaned her backside against the table's edge in a sort of a half-sit. Her go-to power move—casual but strong and deliberate.

She paused as she met the eyes of every individual juror, looked dead at them, and said, simply, "Lawrence Tyler."

Nicki let the name hang in the air while she decided whether to complete the drama or punch it up further. She counted the seconds in her head. After five long seconds, she stood back up, took her hands out of her pockets—she did not want to look too flippant—walked around counsel table back to her seat, and sat down. But not before patting her client gently on the shoulder.

She just sat there. Judge Sullivan was not sure whether to ask Nicki if she was finished and possibly step on a closing argument strategy the likes of which she had never seen, or whether to just call the prosecutor for rebuttal. Nicki was prepared either way.

If Judge Sullivan said, "Counsel, are you finished?" Nicki was prepared to say, "Yes, ma'am." As if nothing unusual at all had happened. Or she would jump back up and give the closing she'd been preparing for days. But some of the jurors began to nod, just slightly, and the judge let the drama and impact of Nicki's gamble settle in. It was a gracious thing for the judge to do, Nicki knew, and she appreciated it. It could have gone a completely different way.

"Mr. Prosecutor," the judge asked, do you have a rebuttal?"

Just as Nicki had bet with herself that she could pull it off, the prosecutor struggled to decide whether to let his trial end on such an extraordinary and surprising note—one that he couldn't possibly mimic—or try to take on what was clearly the most compellingly unimpeachable witness he had ever seen. His case was strong against the other defendants—would he weaken it by trying to raise issues about the case's police detective-turned-CIA-agent star witness? Whom the jury last saw hobbling into the courtroom on crutches. In a partial body cast.

It was smart, he knew, and deliberate that Lawrence Tyler was not in the courtroom for the summations. He was no longer on crutches or in the body cast. The jury would surely have more empathy toward him if they remembered him as he testified, all beat-up looking, than the way he looked now. So, the prosecutor decided to try something in between saying nothing and saying too much.

"Thank you, Your Honor," AUSA Holden began, standing. "Well, you missed out," he continued, trying to take some of the sting out of Nicki's bite. "I've seen some of Ms. Lewis' closing arguments. They *are* stupendous," he continued, gaining back some of the ground Nicki had taken away. "But the most important thing you missed out on is a roadmap—a way to help you evaluate what you heard from Detective Tyler. I believe I can help you. As you deliberate, ask the judge for a standard dictionary. When you get it, look up the definition of an undercover agent. And then decide."

And with that, the prosecutor turned on his heels and sat back down.

Good move, Nicki thought. Whether the judge permitted them to have a dictionary or they looked it up on their own, jurors would see that an undercover agent is defined as someone who uses deceptive techniques in the execution of his or her duties. A liar. Calling Lawrence Tyler a liar directly would most certainly have backfired but implying that someone whose job it is to be deceptive could be less than credible could work. Still, Nicki thought, the move was a gamble. But so was hers.

"Before I instruct you," Judge Sullivan began, "let me ask if any of the jurors need a short break."

None of the jurors needed a break, so Judge Sullivan began her explanation of all the laws that applied to the case and to the jury's deliberation process. Forty-five minutes later, she dismissed the jurors for the night and told them to report to the jury deliberation room at 9:00 the next morning.

"Bold move," Holden said to Nicki as they were packing up their papers and exhibits.

"Yours was clever, too," Nicki said, returning the civility. She generally got along with most of the prosecutors. Even if she thought most of them were dumb as a post, which she often did, she never showed it—not to them. They thought she was a naturally gifted trial lawyer whose native skills could not be taught or learned, and many of them admired how easy she was in the courtroom, no matter the case or the judge. Nicki, of course, thought their admiration was appropriate and deserved.

"Well, I guess we'll see," the prosecutor said.

This was a big case for him. It was already a notorious trial when it began. The unanticipated way it played out made it sensational as well and the proceedings had been reported on every day by all the local news outlets and some national networks. Surely, there would be much to say about the closings, much discussion and dissection.

"Yup," Nicki said. After saying good-bye to her client and stopping to chat with her public defender colleagues—PDSers—in the audience who had come to see her closing, she and her colleagues headed to the haunt they gathered at after a big trial, to drink, lament, and relax. This trial had taken a lot out of Nicki. She thrived on the unpredictability and urgency of trial work, but she didn't feel that she had gotten a good handle on this one. She still didn't know what really happened, how Lawrence Tyler fit into everything, and she didn't believe for a minute that the courtroom shooting was unrelated to the case. She wasn't scared, at least that's what she told herself, but she was unsettled, to be sure. She did not believe the case would end with a verdict, she thought it might hang or mis-try, and she had a gnawing feeling something else bad was going to happen. Plus, she thought someone was following her.

"The jury's out," Agent Stackhouse said to the President later that night.

The President had asked Agent Stackhouse to keep him informed when Nicki's case wrapped up. It was important, the President thought, that anything and everything related to the project he was working on be fully resolved, and the F Street case had become an extraordinarily unforeseen, shocking, and sad part of it.

"I heard. Did Judge Sullivan do her usual impeccable job with instructions?"

"Yes, that's the word."

"Okay. Let me know when you hear something."

"Yes, Mr. President."

"You all right?"

"Fine, sir. How's Abby?"

"The light of my life. As always."

"Goodnight, Mr. President."

"Goodnight, Agent Stackhouse."

"I thought you had to work tonight," Tommie said, sliding her right arm around David's waist and standing on her toes to kiss him on the mouth.

It had startled her to hear the doorbell ring and to look out the window and see David's sleek, black government car. She raced to the bathroom to check her face and hair. David didn't like doing that—using his government car for unrelated activities, it was against the rules. But it was late, and he would have had to drive forty-five minutes home and then thirty minutes back to Tommie's. He did not like imposing on her like that either, but this night he needed to be with her, and he didn't care if he was seen there.

"How was your day?" David asked.

"We had a funny moment on the chiefs of staff call this morning."

"What did you do?"

"How do you know I did something?" Tommie laughed.

"I can tell when you're being devious, you should know that by now."

"Okay, so remember when I told you there is a chief on the morning call who either falls asleep and snores really loud, or has a serious breathing issue, and it sounds like the Darth Vader voice? Well, I conspired with one of the other chiefs who does a spot-on Darth Vader—and President, by the way—to get on the call and say *'Luke, I am your faaaather, come to the dark side...'*" Tommie was cracking up at herself. "But the snore-y guy, he didn't get it, so we still don't know who he is, and he kept breathing really loud the rest of the call."

"I can't believe you guys did that on the call. Isn't that the daily 7:30 call where the White House tells all the executive branch agency chiefs of staff what the President and Vice-President are doing that day, what the White House message is for the day, what they want you to do to push the President's agenda?"

"Yeah."

"And you tell them anything important about what your secretaries are doing, and they give you guys a heads-up about anything critical?"

"Yeah, and?"

"*Tsk, tsk,*" David said feigning indignation. "If the President only knew how his chiefs were behaving—"

"Hey! We have to have *some* fun!" Tommie said, still laughing. "Anyway, how are you? How was your day?"

"Long day."

"Are you hungry, have you eaten yet?"

"No, but I'm not hungry. My stomach is bothering me."

"Are you staying?" Tommie headed to the kitchen. "Want some water?"

"Yes, thanks." David followed her up the stairs to the bedroom. "Do you want to watch Colbert?"

"Sure."

Tommie began taking the decorative pillows off the bed. David sat at the foot of the bed and took his shoes off. Tommie scooched up behind him, straddling his hips with her legs, and began to massage his lower back with both hands. David dropped his head back and let out a quiet moan. Tommie ran her hands up and down his back, over his shoulders and down the front of his chest, kissing his neck. In one motion, he grabbed her right arm and pulled her around until she was lying face up across his lap. He reached down and put his mouth on hers, holding her more tightly than usual. He kissed her, slowly, gently, as though he was learning her for the first time, then rolled her back around on the bed, sliding her arms above her head and locking his fingers in her hands.

"I missed you today," David said.

"I can see that," Tommie whispered.

They stayed that way for a long time, lying across the foot of the bed, kissing. Tommie felt so relaxed—and safe—that she almost dozed off.

"You're falling asleep!" David said feigning insult.

"Hhmm," Tommie moaned.

"Let's get under the covers."

"Let's just lie right here and kiss."

"Come on, get in," David said, pulling back the covers.

"All of a sudden, I feel so sleepy," Tommie said. "You've probably drugged me with some experimental drug."

"What, with my tongue? Wouldn't I be falling asleep too?"

"I don't know. It's your drug. You probably made it so it rubbed off from you to me without affecting you."

"You are *so* silly," David said now pulling Tommie on top of him under the sheet and kissing her neck.

"I thought you said you were tired."

"I thought *you* were sleepy from the drugs."

"They seem to be having a different effect now," Tommie said, moving her mouth down his stomach, past his navel.

"I can see that," David said, barely audible except for the sound of his mouth pulling the air in through his teeth.

CHAPTER NINETEEN

A couple of days later, after the jury went out, Nicki was drinking wine and nodding off when the doorbell rang. She got up from the couch, tossed Stoli off the arm rest, and looked out the front window. There was no car in sight but there's no parking on her side of the street, and it would be impossible to know if a visitor was parked up or down the block. Her friends all knew to call before they came over because she was unlikely to answer the door for anyone at night, and Shep was out of town. But the face she saw through the peep hole, albeit elongated and zig-zaggy from the old glass, looked friendly, if not familiar.

"Who is it?" Nicki called through the door, "and what the hell are you doing ringing my doorbell?"

"Nik, it's me," the voice answered. Nicki was getting ready to make a smart remark when suddenly she could hardly take in the air in front of her. No one called her Nik. Not Shep. Not her mother. Not her best friend. No one except . . .

"Please, Nik, let me in. I need to talk to you," Detective Tyler was saying to the door.

Nicki opened the door slowly, peering through the sliver of space she allowed.

"What do you want? I'm not in the mood," Nicki said holding the door. Tyler caught Niki's hand as he reached toward the handle.

"I owe you a lot of explaining Nik, I know," he said taking a step into the foyer but not going beyond the invisible line that separates a welcomed guest from someone you would just as soon dispatch at the threshold. "And I will, but right now I need to talk to you. Somewhere private."

"Fine, go ahead," Nicki said trying not to reveal her complicated feelings. Right now, she was mostly pissed off, so much so that her good home training failed to offer her guest a seat, or even something to drink. She just stood there with him in the foyer, arms folded across her chest. "What?"

"It's not private here, Nik."

"What do you mean it's not private? No bugs here the last time I did a sweep." She was being facetious; she never swept for bugs. That was television shit.

"There are, and when was the last time you checked?" Detective Tyler asked. He was not being facetious.

"This is my *home*."

"I know, Nik. Grab a jacket. It will be cold."

It was not Nicki's nature to let things go. She should have been asking a million questions. *What the hell is going on? Who bugged my house? When? How? Where? Why? Where the hell are we going? Are you kidding me with this cloak and dagger crap? Should I have asked for a mistrial?*

Her mind raced wildly from thought to thought and she was still angry that after all these years Tyler had the nerve to show up at her house, unannounced. *He knows I hate that!* But Nicki didn't say any of that out loud. Instead, she grabbed a jacket, a cell phone, and identification, and followed Lawrence Tyler out the front door, around the side of the house where Tyler stopped, motioned to be quiet, and looked down at his watch ... 8, 7, 6, 5, 4, 3, 2, 1, his digital wrist computer counted down. It was not an ordinary watch, Nicki noticed, and on zero a black van screeched around the corner practically on two wheels. Tyler grabbed Nicki's hand and bolted for the van. Nicki could see that there was no open door and if they kept running as fast as they were going, they were going to crack their heads open slamming into the side of the van. Just as she closed her eyes, the side door slid open, and in one motion both Detective Tyler and Nicki were in a heap on the floor of the van, and Tyler was yelling "Go, go, go, go, go!"

"You all right?" Tyler asked.

Nicki just nodded. What was she going to say now that she'd already bought into whatever was happening?

I'm uncomfortable with all of this? I think I might have broken my pinky, she thought. She was still mad, but now she was also scared.

They drove for only a short time. By the twists and turns, Nicki assumed they were somewhere in Rock Creek Park near her house. Just as the van began to slow down, Tyler glanced at the lighted round thing on his wrist, pushed something in that made a beeping noise, and then held a button down until the light turned from white to blue.

"We're here," Tyler said to the thing on his wrist and just then the doors opened, and Nicki saw a suited arm extend a hand.

"Big step," the voice said.

"Good to see you, David," Tyler said.

"Likewise LT, Ms. Lewis," Agent Stackhouse said nodding his greeting and helping Nicki out of the van.

"What the fuck—" Nicki recognized Agent Stackhouse from television shots of President Pierce as the first Black man ever to head the President's Secret Service detail. "Sorry . . . what the *hell* is going on here?"

"We'll tell you what we can, Ms. Lewis," Agent Stackhouse said leading them both past the horse stables in Rock Creek Park and towards the water.

CHAPTER TWENTY

Earlier that day something happened during jury deliberations. Judge Sullivan could always tell by the way her lead marshal, Sam Waithe, was knocking at her chamber's door.

"Come in, Sam," Judge Sullivan said before Sam could identify himself.

"It's Sam, Your Honor," he said even though the judge had already spoken to him by name. Sam still thought it was proper to identify himself. He knew how illogical it must have sounded to her, day after day, for her to say, "come in Sam," and him to say, "it's Sam, Your Honor." But that was their thing. Another one of their things.

"The jury has a note," Sam told her.

"What does it say?" Judge Sullivan was joking. Sam was far too by-the-book ever to read a jury's note, or a verdict, or do anything improper.

Sam smiled. "Your Honor, you know I never read the jury's notes."

"Yes Sam, I know," the judge smiled as she took the note from Sam. "I'll call you when I'm ready."

"Yes, ma'am. I hope you had a restful evening."

"I did Sam, thank you," Judge Sullivan lied. She had tossed and turned all night, waking up several times from disturbing dreams and sounds she kept hearing around her home. *It's nothing,* she kept telling herself, but she wasn't convinced she was just hearing things go bump in the night, and she almost called Sam more than once. It had happened once before when she had presided over a difficult, controversial public trial. That time, someone tried to break into her house to intimidate her, or worse. It was a mob case at a time when the "families" had no compunction about killing judges, and the Justice Department let six cases get by it before they could turn a "capo," find out who was ordering the hits, and get the murders stopped. There was a lot of bloodshed during that time. Two of Judge Sullivan's close colleagues were gunned down execution style. She was sorry for them, and their families, but grateful the bloodshed was not hers or any of the marshals who had been assigned to protect her. Particularly Sam. She never got all the way through, in her head, the practice conversation where she had to tell Sam's wife that he had been killed in the line of duty. She just couldn't imagine ever being able to do it.

The jury's note was uneventful. They wanted to know if they could use a dictionary and they wanted to have lunch earlier that day. The judge buzzed Sam and told him to give the jury an Oxford dictionary and ask them how early they wanted lunch. A few minutes later, Sam buzzed back and told her they had changed their mind about the dictionary, that they had figured it out, and that they wanted to eat at 11:30, if that wasn't too early. Judge Sullivan was convinced the jury had a verdict. The evidence against the defendants was almost overwhelming, three days of deliberation for a few defendants was a respectable amount of time, and if they got their verdict in by two or so, they would all be home with their families in time for dinner. But she'd misjudged a jury's actions before, so she didn't make plans for the early evening this time, the way she had the time when the jury ended up sending eleven more notes before they hung.

"Sam, what do you think?" Judge Sullivan goaded the Marshal.

"I think they want to eat," Sam said, laughing with the judge.

"They always want to eat."

Nicki could hardly see anything where she, Detective Tyler, and Agent Stackhouse were standing. She could hear the creek, but the darkness made it hard to tell how far away it was. It could have been a foot in front of her, for all she knew. She could have been standing in it, as cold as she was.

I should have grabbed a heavier jacket, Nicki thought.

"Ms. Lewis, I am Special Agent David Stackhouse. I work for President Pierce."

"I know who you are," Nicki snapped—though not sarcastically, which would have been her way in other circumstances.

"I will tell you what I can that involves you. First, we know that you are being watched, followed, and that your home has been fitted with listening and visual devices."

I thought someone was following me!

"We're pretty sure we know who it is, and why. As strange as this will sound, you have never been in any danger. We have been keeping close tabs on the people who are watching you," Agent Stackhouse explained.

"So, these 'people,' and the Secret Service, have been watching me and listening to everything I've been saying?" Nicki said. She was incredulous, and now quite frightened.

"Not exactly. We have been respectful of your privacy."

"The fu—," Nicki cleared her throat and tried again. "What the hell does that mean?"

"It means we have recorded their recordings, both listening and visual, but we have neither reviewed or viewed the tapes. We would not do that in this case unless you gave us your express permission, and right now, we don't think it will be necessary to ask you for it."

"Why not?"

"Well, as I said, we believe we know who has targeted you and why. Unless something we have not uncovered arises, we can take the appropriate investigative actions with what we already know without learning more from the tapes."

"I assume it has to do with this trial, and Lawrence's secret identity shit." Nicki negotiated with herself. Given the complications of the situation and her anger, "shit" was just fine to say. It was fact after all; what Lawrence had pulled was indeed *shit*.

"Yes, although we won't be able to tell you much more about Mr. Tyler's work than you have already learned through the trial."

"Well, what am I supposed to do now? How am I supposed to feel comfortable in my own home? What, am I going to have to sleep in my office now?"

Nicki knew, from the looks on Agent Stackhouse's and Detective Tyler's faces, that her office must have be under surveillance too.

"They've bugged my office too, haven't they?" she said, cutting Agent Stackhouse off before he had a chance to tell her exactly that.

"Yes, ma'am."

"What is up with this ma'am shit you guys do all the time?"

Now the whole thing was shit as far as Nicki was concerned. It was a throw-away question. She did not expect an answer; she was just tired.

"Ms. Lewis, we are going to need you to try to continue as if nothing is going on. We believe that at this moment, if you signal that you know anything, we may not be able to get to you fast enough to protect you. The only place in your home where you can speak without being heard is in your foyer.

"If you want to have a private conversation, we suggest you casually move to that area while you're talking."

"What do I do about showering and things like that?"

"As long as you pull the shower curtains all the way closed, you can't be seen. But you can be heard." Agent Stackhouse hoped Nicki could hear the empathy in his voice.

Nicki sighed. "Why is whoever doing this, doing this?"

"They think you might know what I know," Detective Tyler said.

"Well, that's ironic," Nicki said. She was spent. "I didn't even recognize you during the trial."

"We think they have enough from the tapes to know you have not actually been in contact with Detective Tyler for some time," Agent Stackhouse said. "But they didn't know that before. It's possible that once the verdict comes in, they will back off. Once they verify that there is no communication between you."

"What if there is no verdict? What if they hang?"

"Then we'll meet again, Ms. Lewis, and figure out things from there," Agent Stackhouse said.

"You're shivering," Detective Tyler said. "Here, put my jacket over your shoulders." He stepped behind Agent Stackhouse and around to Nicki.

"We should head back," Agent Stackhouse said. And just then a sleek black sedan with way too many antennas even for a police car came out of nowhere to whisk Nicki away.

"Don't let anything happen to her," Detective Tyler said to Stackhouse as they headed for their respective vehicles.

"You have my word," Stackhouse assured.

Detective Tyler had not known Agent Stackhouse long, only a year or so, but he was certain that whatever Stackhouse said you could take to the bank.

CHAPTER TWENTY-ONE

"Hear ye, hear ye, the court will now come back to order," the clerk announced. "Judge Sullivan presiding."

"I've reconvened this matter," Judge Sullivan began, "to make the following announcements and offer the following opinions. For the record, counsel has already been informed in chambers. First, I am extremely sorry to inform you that juror number seven has died. Apparently, he died last evening in his sleep of what investigators are calling 'natural causes.' I have polled the jurors individually and at length and their preference was to proceed with their deliberations, which they have done, and they have informed me that they indeed have a verdict."

The courtroom was completely hushed. "Mr. Marshal, would you please receive the verdict?"

Marshal Sam Waithe received the verdict from the alternate foreman and handed it to the judge.

"As to defendant Williams," the judge began, "on the charge of armed and aggravated assault with intent to kill, the jury has found you guilty. As to defendant Williams, on the charge of aggravated sodomy, the jury has found you guilty. As to defendant Williams, on the charge of first-degree murder with special circumstances, the jury has found you guilty."

On hearing that last guilty verdict, members of the victim's family began to cry tears of relief and sorrow. And that's how it continued for each of the three male defendants—guilty verdicts across the board, the main charges of murder and all the accompanying charges prosecutors add on—with each member of the victim's family discharging the depth of their despair upon each murder conviction.

It took Judge Sullivan almost ten minutes to get through all the charges for each of the three defendants. None of them moved, or made a sound, or even looked up. Not even when the judge said "special circumstances"—words they all knew meant life in prison without the possibility of parole.

"As to defendant Miss Gray, on the charge of armed and aggravated assault, the jury finds you not guilty. As to defendant Miss Gray, on the charge of aggravated sodomy, the jury finds you not guilty. As to defendant Miss Gray, on the charge of first-degree murder with special circumstances, the jury finds you not guilty."

Before the judge could thank and release the jury, or set the sentencing dates for the convicted defendants, the courtroom became a confluence of conflicting noises competing for time and space; cell phone dialing, laptop keyboard clicking, whispers, tears, the sound of a bunch of lawyers returning legal pads to their briefcases and giving instructions to the baby lawyers who were in charge of the physical evidence and exhibits. As Nicki was shaking congratulatory hands of colleagues and friends, she turned her body slightly, just enough to get in the line of sight. And there he was. Agent Stackhouse, slipping through what she had thought, through the whole trial, was a wall.

"He's waiting for you," the President's personal secretary, Julia, said to Agent Stackhouse.

"How's he feeling?" Agent Stackhouse asked. Julia well knew he was checking the President's mood, not his health.

"Abby's in there."

The President was always in a terrific mood when he had Abby. The few people who knew about, and protected, the secrecy of Abby all knew that.

The entire planet could have begun World War III, but as long as Abby was safe and happy, the President believed all was right with the world.

Sometimes the few top aides who knew Abby would wait for the President to be with her before they brought him bad news. It made for an easier, and less loud, conversation. They had thought they were being clever, but the President caught on to it a long time ago and he would note which of the few aides tried to use the old trick. Then, when the aide was most off-guard, usually a time when Abby was in the Oval Office and they were delivering bad news, the President would say, "Abby, tell Mr. so-and-so aide how you feel about him giving me bad news when you're in here with me." And with that Abby would answer *"phtttttttr"* with her tongue. The President would stand stoic for what seemed like an unbearable amount of time, and then Abby would collapse in a fit of giggles. The President would smile, but it was not until the President winked at that aide that the aide took a breath again—by then he or she was almost hyperventilating from holding it so long.

The President enjoyed the times he could make light of the dead seriousness of West Wing life with some of his top aides, and he hoped it rubbed off a little. Abby, of course, was too young to take any of it seriously and he enjoyed having such a willing, innocent, and unaware participant in his mischief.

"Mr. President," Agent Stackhouse said nodding as he entered the Oval Office. Abby was already gone, he noted.

The President only has her leave at the most serious of times, Stackhouse thought. *He should be happy. The trial is over, Abby is with him, the press inquiries into the fires have abated, somewhat at least. What's wrong now?*

"David," the President said, "have a seat. Can I get you anything to drink? Are you hungry?"

"No, sir, I'm fine."

President Pierce nodded. "Interesting result with the trial."

"Not unexpected, given the testimony. I supposed there would be more of a commotion about the verdict, given how much commotion there was throughout the trial."

What is the President digging at? Stackhouse thought.

"Well, I'm glad it's over. I hope it stays that way. Anything to report on that other matter we discussed?"

"We have uncovered no information that would confirm the concerns or fears of the Homeland Security Secretary," Agent Stackhouse responded. "I don't believe we will need to revisit the issue the Homeland Security Secretary raised with you that day."

It had been a complicated undertaking to track down the rumors about the White House's involvement in a scandalous event, but it had been accomplished quickly and without resort to radical measures. Agent Stackhouse had to call in a chit for the information, something he hated doing, but it was worth it because the information was reliable, and it answered all the questions. It started with activity that was abandoned by a political rival and picked up by a guy who was pretty much a nut but smart enough to have wrangled his way to a White House Christmas party invite—which had him mixing, mingling, and spreading rumors to influential political and media types, intimating that President Pierce was involved in a behind-the-scenes deal with Pakistan in violation of the Camp David accords. This guy's deception was so thorough and complete it first appeared that he was working with people of import. Rather, it was a manifestation of the pervasiveness of his mental disturbance that enabled his scheme to appear so calculated and absolute. In any event, Agent Stackhouse was glad that this, too, was over, even more than the trial. His hands were all over this one.

"Good work," President Pierce said. The buzzer sounded then. "Yes, Julia?"

"Your four o'clock is ready, sir."

"I need a few more minutes."

"No problem, sir," Agent Stackhouse said, "I need to be getting back anyway."

It did not look like the President was going to ask for details about the findings, or the agency's methods of investigation, but Agent Stackhouse wanted to get out of there before he thought of doing so. He reached out to shake the President's hand goodbye, but the President pulled his arm close in and gave him the one-armed back pat handshake acknowledgement.

"Thanks," the President said quietly. "It's nice to have the trial issues, and your review, behind us. How much longer do you think the media will continue to pursue the U Street matter?"

"Frankly, I believe someone will chase that for years to come. At least the networks are starting to lose interest; Police Chief Coley and Fire Chief Ramsey did a good job of preventing leaks," Agent Stackhouse said, getting in a good plug for his friend.

"Please pass along my thanks to Jim," the President said.

"Of course, sir. He will appreciate that."

"Are his people doing any better? He lost a couple of them because of this, didn't he?"

"Yes sir, he did. Two to early retirement, one to mental disability. Hopefully, it will be temporary."

"Well, let's figure out some way to publicly recognize all of the men and women involved in the U Street investigation."

"That may well renew press interest, particularly if you are publicly involved, Mr. President."

"You're right. Well, talk to the police chief about a private ceremony with bonus awards, promotions, whatever is appropriate."

"I'd prefer you not get involved even in suggesting details, Mr. President. I'd like to keep you as far away from U Street as possible. Plus, your chief of staff would try to tear me a new one if I supported your involvement, even in an honorary event."

They both laughed.

"Mr. President," Agent Stackhouse said, seriously. "I know, we all know, you are concerned and appreciative of the team's efforts. I will make sure the police chief understands the depth of your gratefulness; we'll work it out."

"Thank you, again."

"Of course, Mr. President." Agent Stackhouse turned to leave. "Tell Abby I said, *'See you later alligator.'*"

"Of course, David. Julia?" the President said into the intercom. "I'm ready for Sheila."

The President and Sheila, Abby's mother, spoke on a regular schedule once a month, more if things came up with Abby. No one knew about this except Julia and Agent Stackhouse. Both the President and Sheila preferred it that way. It was way too complicated a situation to explain to anyone else, and far too personal to risk leaks. They remained very good friends even though Sheila waited until after Abby was born to tell the President about her, and their love for their daughter made their close bond even stronger. They checked in with each other every month on the same day and at the same time, no matter what else was going on in the world. The President enjoyed his conversations with Sheila. They gave him insights into his beloved daughter that he could not pick up in the limited days and hours he had with her. He also liked talking with Sheila. They had had a powerful, passionate relationship before Abby was conceived, and he had missed her when she secretly went away to have Abby. They could talk to each other about anything and he trusted her. He had never worried that she would reveal their secret, and not just because of her own professional reputation.

"Hello, Sheila," the President said into his private line, "I'm sorry I kept you waiting. How are you?"

"I'm well, Clifford. Busy. It's a busy time, as you know."

"Yes, the silly season, as the journalists call it." The President laughed.

"Not silly to me," Sheila replied. "It's how I eat. How are you doing, Clifford, really? A lot has happened in the past month, or so I read."

"Yes, it's been eventful around here. It *has* been tough. But it looks like things are quieting down. I think. I hope. I can't share much more than that about this one though Sheila, I'm sorry."

"You know you don't have to apologize to me. I understand. Just want to make sure you remember my number when you need an ear."

"I know. And knowing that lifts me when I'm down—even when I don't reach out to you. I hope *you* know that."

"Yes. I do."

"So, how's my girl doing? She seems fine when she is here. She runs and jumps and plays around the Oval Office when I'm working alone, and she likes to pretend she can hide from me in the residence after hours."

"She absolutely adores you, and she is truly happy and at peace when she is with you. When she comes back, it's like she's been to see the wizard and gotten all of her wishes granted."

"I'm glad to hear that. With all that has been going on, I was afraid the darkness of it might have been dripping off me and splashing onto her a little bit."

"No, no, don't worry about that. I would tell you."

But she wasn't telling him. She had decided not to tell the President that Abby had started having "scare-ring dreams" as Abby called them. Sheila had spoken to a child psychologist about them and was comfortable that it was just a phase she would grow out of as she got older and adjusted more fully to her parents living in separate houses. Bad dreams were a very typical response in kids Abby's age, all the experts said, and Sheila believed the right thing to do was to ride the phase out before talking to Clifford about it.

"How's the practice going?" the President asked. He asked that every month. He always had a good sense of what Sheila was doing even before they talked; she was a well-known lobbyist and the issues she worked on sometimes made news.

"Your policies keep me in high cotton," Sheila joked. "Someone is always for *or* against them."

"Well, you know that's the only reason why I ran," he joked back. "To keep you in high cotton."

"Well, keep it up!" Sheila was trying to prolong the moment they were enjoying.

"Perhaps I will make that my campaign theme when I run for re-election. 'Keep it up!' I think the American people would like that. It's bold, optimistic."

"You say that as a joke, but I bet you all the money your hard-fought policies have earned me that those words will somehow make their way in one of your speeches." Their playfulness paused. Sheila continued, "It's nice to hear your voice Clifford, as always. Do call me if you need to." She was always mindful of the President's time.

"I will," the President answered. "But you know what they say, 'be careful what you wish for.'"

"*You* know what they say Clifford; 'you don't ask, you don't get.'"

They always ended their phone calls this way, using some quote or old saying to speak the words they never uttered anymore: *I still love you.*

CHAPTER TWENTY-TWO

Nicki was pleased, though not surprised, that her client was acquitted, and the other defendants found guilty. It was a rare circumstance, certainly.

Just as well, given all the other things that had happened in that courtroom, Nicki thought.

Still, she felt uneasy. The Secret Service had assured her that they removed all their surveillance equipment, that they no longer thought she was in danger, that they were no longer concerned about her safety. But she was uncomfortable. After Secret Service technicians had been through her house and office removing all of their paraphernalia, she had gone around her entire house, and office, looking for anything unusual. She knew she was not expert enough to detect anything someone wanted to hide, but she did it anyway. She even asked a police lieutenant friend of hers to do a walk-through for her; when he'd turned up empty-handed, Nicki had asked Shep. But he didn't find anything he thought was surveillance equipment, either.

Nicki was troubled by all the things that happened the night Detective Tyler showed up at her house—how she was whisked away in the dark as if she were in a thriller. And she was unsatisfied with what she was told. They didn't tell her anything, not really. She didn't buy the national security argument they gave her; she had never trusted the government to do anything honestly, and she believed even less in the representations the government made in its official capacity. She had been intensely proud and filled with emotion when Agent Stackhouse was first asked by the President to head his protective detail, but she found herself questioning whether this smart, intellectually and physically imposing Black man, who carried the weight of the world's superpower on his shoulders, had not been compromised in some way by the might of the man. She still could not believe they went through all that cloak and dagger stuff to tell her basically nothing, and she hadn't heard a thing from LT since that night.

Maybe he wanted to make sure his presence didn't put her in an awkward position while she was waiting for the verdict.

It didn't matter. The whole thing was way too screwed up, and she was tired of feeling disconcerted. All she wanted to do was watch something mindless on TV, finish off that bottle of pinot grigio, and relax in her favorite chair. She had enjoyed hanging out with her PDS colleagues at the bar across the street from the courthouse after the verdict, but now she just wanted to get out of her court clothes and into the sweats she wouldn't wear even to grab the newspaper off the stoop. She popped a bag of microwave popcorn, locked all the doors in the house, turned the ringer off the phone and settled into an *I Love Lucy* marathon.

She was just starting to watch the classic episode where Lucy and Ethel have jobs at the chocolate factory (the one where the conveyor is faster than their ability to wrap the pieces) when the cat suddenly woke up and began hissing in the direction of the door. Nicki wasn't sure whether to feel scared or put out. She decided put out was a better emotional state than scared, so she relaxed into that emotion, got up with determination and grit, and walked toward the door with stubborn impatience. She walked quietly, however, hoping not to reveal her presence in the house, and she put her eye to the peephole without touching the door. The doorbell rang out, startling her.

"Who is it?"

"Nik, it's me again," Detective Tyler answered. "Sorry if I startled you, no one answered the phone."

"Come in," Nicki said surprised at her own relief.

Detective Tyler looked tired, Nicki noticed, and was no longer acting like he was in a spy novel. He followed her into the family room and slunk into a chair across from hers.

"Have a seat," Nicki said, and Detective Tyler managed a smile. "Can I get you anything?"

"Do you have any scotch?"

"Yes, rocks?"

"Straight is fine, I don't want you to go to any trouble."

"No trouble," Nicki said, plunking a couple of ice cubes into an oversized tumbler. Detective Tyler sat there for a while, sinking further into his seat, taking in the scotch in long quiet sips. To Nicki it felt like the life that filled the space between the last time she was with him, and this moment, never happened. That she was face-to-face, again, with the man she had thought she would love forever.

"Congratulations on the verdict," Detective Tyler said.

"Thank you." Nicki sneaked a quick peek at the show before turning the television down.

"How do you feel?"

"About the verdict, things generally, what do you mean?"

"About the trial, the verdict."

"Oh, well good of course. Not surprised, but good." Nicki wondered how long they would be making small talk and how soon she could ask him directly what he wanted.

"I loved your closing," Detective Tyler said.

"Of course you loved it," Nicki laughed. "It was all about you. It *was* you!"

"Well, there is that." He pulled himself up straighter in the chair and smoothed his hair. "How is your client?" he asked.

Just then, Nicki recalled that she didn't recall seeing Tyler in the courtroom during the closing arguments. She wasn't up for playing twenty questions, though.

"She's fine. Not overwhelmingly grateful, I would opine."

"She should be the most grateful person on the planet. But I remember how the defendants were. You could see it from our side too—the indifference, the sense of entitlement. I always wondered how you guys worked that hard and long for people, many of whom were guilty, for so little return."

"You, my mother, and half the world. But you know how that goes. For every one of you guys, the ones that try to be fair, there are five cops who are driven by the wrong outcomes, who are corrupt . . . or worse."

"Yeah . . . " Tyler said, his voice fading off. "I didn't miss that aspect of the job when I—"

"What happened to you? Where did you go?" Nicki interrupted him with a quick harsh tone but then lowered it on the second question, feeling the weight of her curiosity. "You look quite different now."

"Nik, I can't." A long time passed in the silence that ended his answer. "I still can't say any more than I already have."

"Then why are you here?" She crossed her arms quickly.

"I wanted to see . . . to check on you. Make sure you were all right. Tell you that this is over."

Now Detective Tyler was out of his chair, walking around the room, looking out the window, looking at nothing.

"It's over? *What* is over? What the fuck is the *it*? Like I told Agent Stackhouse, I don't believe in all this cloak and dagger shit. I am a taxpaying United States citizen, I work hard, I deserve better than to have gone through all of this and then have the government just say, 'sorry, national security, can't tell you.'"

"That's how it works Nik, unfortunately. You'd probably think I was a chump or something if you knew the activities I have involved myself in knowing just a fraction of the whole story."

"I probably *would* think you were a chump, but that was a choice you made. I didn't have any choice being put in the middle of all of this. I really think someone owes me an explanation."

"An explanation would endanger your life, Nik, and I don't intend for that to happen. People already mistakenly thought you were involved in something you weren't, and we had to protect you from them. Either that or they just diverted some of our resources," Tyler said, now talking as if he was debating that thought with himself. "Either way, aside from all the 'cloak and dagger shit,'" he smiled at Nicki's phrasing, "it's just too dangerous. I'd prefer you be angry at me for the rest of our lives than put you in that position."

"I'm already mad at you for the rest of our lives," Nicki said, lightening a little. "You have a way of not explaining things, remember?"

Nicki did not want to drudge up their interrupted past, but she knew him well enough, she thought, that the conversation was not going to end satisfactorily. She was not going to learn any more than she knew already, no matter her hurt. Or indignation.

"You know," Nicki said, "I'm getting tired. I think the weight of everything is starting to come down on me. Suddenly, I feel very sleepy."

She *was* tired. She could feel the adrenaline that keeps a trial lawyer going through a trial on little sleep draining from her body.

"I understand," Detective Tyler, said quickly picking up his jacket and moving towards the foyer. He knew too that while she was starting to crash from the roar of the past couple of months, she was mostly tired of the dance—with him. They both knew it was not leading anywhere.

"Take care of yourself, Nik," he said softly at the door. "Take my cell, call me if you ever need anything."

Nicki took the scrap of paper Detective Tyler had scribbled a number on.

"This is local?" Nicki asked more than stated. "Are you going to be back in the area for a while?"

"It can find me anywhere in the world," he said, his voice lowering again.

"Oh. Well, you're still handsome."

That was out of the blue, Detective Tyler thought.

"You don't look so bad yourself."

Tyler wanted to tell her how weird and scary it had been to go under the knife, to change who he was from the outside in. He wanted to tell her how lonely he had been in a world where he had a different history from his own memories, why he couldn't call her, why he couldn't even inquire about her. He did not regret making the choice, taking on the assignment, but he underestimated the lasting affect it would have on his family, his friends, himself. Thousands had done it before him. Men and women. And there were a few stories of operatives taking a dive off a bridge in despair. The toll was high. The proscription against talking with anyone about your experiences—with your colleagues, even with the decompression counselor assigned to you—drops you in a depth of aloneness that you can't work out, not in your head, not in your heart.

It's too late for all of that, he thought. *I need to just keep moving.*

Nicki was surprised at her level of dissatisfaction. She was not naïve enough to think the man she knew as LT was just going to pour his heart out and tell her everything. The way things had gone were much too grave for that. But she did not like to think she lived in a country where such grave things could go ... unanswered, unrequited. She picked up Stoli, who had reappeared from her hiding spot, hugged her to her face, and headed for the kitchen.

"This is a funny, funny world," Nicki said to her companion. "You're smart. You just stay inside and are warm and dry and you get fed and you don't worry about all the crazies or all the craziness. In my next life, I'm going to come back as one of you guys, and I'm going to be with people when I want and snub them when I feel like it, and otherwise just... be." Nicki chuckled at herself for the silly, long, soliloquy she had just given. To a cat.

CHAPTER TWENTY-THREE

The phone rang just as Nicki was putting Stoli down on the counter where she liked to sit and watch Nicki busy herself in the kitchen.

"Hello?" she answered, not remembering to check the caller ID first.

"Nicki, it's Reggie Stone. I called to congratulate you."

"Reggie!" Nicki exclaimed, "you son of a—how are you? Where are you?"

"I'm in your city," Reggie said. "Heard about everything on the news. Are you up for a drink or are you in for the night?"

"I'm up. Where?"

"I'm staying at the Jurys Washington Hotel; you know it?"

"Oh, that's poetic, don't you think?" Nicki said. "Are you serious?"

"Yup, they do a lot of conference work. I'm here for an American Bar Association conference," Reggie laughed. "It's right at DuPont Circle."

"Yup, I know it. See you in twenty?"

"Perfect. See you then. Nicki," Reggie said pausing. "I'm glad I caught you. I wanted to buy you a drink tonight."

"Drinks. Plural," Nicki said chuckling. She didn't want to start out an evening with her old friend feeling mushy and sentimental. She just wanted to have fun. And forget about LT.

"Plural. You got it. See you soon."

Reggie had worked at PDS too. He was so comfortable in the courtroom you could almost picture him in a robe and bedroom slippers just hanging out and chatting in the big chair in his den rather than sitting at counsel table. He was the first lawyer to come to PDS in a long time who matched Nicki's smoothness.

When Nicki arrived, Reggie was sitting at the far end of the bar. It was crowded for a weeknight, and she figured all the suits were lawyers trying to liquidate their daily trials and troubles.

Hey, that's like three corny puns, she thought as she walked toward Reggie, smiling.

"Well, you're no worse for wear, I see," Reggie said rising from the stool and giving Nicki a long, solid hug, kissing her on both cheeks.

"So, we're French now?" Nicki joked right away.

They always ragged on each other for the first ten or fifteen minutes, longer if it had been a while. Reggie was older and more experienced than Nicki, but when they both ended up public defenders in Washington, D.C. together, everyone seemed to treat them as if they were equals. Nicki never thought they were equals. She always believed, and behaved, in a way that demonstrated her respect for his commitment to that kind of work, and for his skills as a trial lawyer which, though not as well known, were superior. At least in her view.

"Why didn't you find the most remote stools in the whole bar like we're lovers having a secret rendezvous?" she continued to tease, settling into her stool beside him.

"You wish," Reggie laughed. I know you've been secretly after me for years. That's why I moved to Cleveland. It was pathetic watching you pine over me."

"Me? Who's the one in that picture of all of us at Hooligan's that time? Everyone's looking at stupid Bernie taking the picture and you're looking down my blouse! It's a good thing you never wanted to run for anything! I could have blackmailed you blind!"

"Hey! Bernie doctored that picture, that son-of-a-bitch!" Reggie said. And that's how it went for a while.

Reggie was drinking a ginger ale when Nicki had first arrived, but he switched to a scotch and soda when Nicki ordered hers. She had taken a cab to the hotel from her house, something she often did when she knew she would be drinking.

"So, tell me about the conference," Nicki said easing her way into a real conversation.

"Same ol' same ol'," Reggie said. "You know I'm heading this ABA Taskforce on Judicial Independence, right?"

"Right, right."

"I'm presenting the task force's preliminary results at the conference tomorrow afternoon. I can get you in. You should come."

Nicki nodded noncommittally. "So, what's the deal? Is our judiciary independent enough or not?"

Judicial independence had been a topic that PDS lawyers debated all the time. So many of the judges in D.C. Superior Court and U.S. District Court were former prosecutors, and former public defenders almost never made it on the bench. The one or two who did make it took longer to advance to District Court, even though there was no discernable evidence that they were less qualified or more lenient. There was discernable evidence, though, that former prosecutors imposed much tougher sentences than any other judges, and while no one could prove it, no one could disprove the existence of a feeder program from the U.S. Attorney's office to a D.C. judgeship.

"I am chagrined to report that there is a lack of independence serious enough in some states to call into question more than twenty percent of all sentences imposed in criminal cases across the country," Reggie answered.

"Wow," Nicki said. "I didn't think they would be able to make a direct link."

"Link they did." He said this in a register just audible in the busy bar. "I'll send you our paper on it, our finding, and you can read it at your leisure," Reggie said, trying to change the subject. "Now, tell me about this crazy trial. I can't believe the case even got to the jury. The appeal grounds on either side are going to be some law professor's dream case study one day."

"Yeah, you'd think that. I'm not so sure," Nicki began. "As crazy as all that shit was, the facts were the facts, the witnesses were the witnesses. If you parse through all that madness, none of it changed what happened that night in that alley."

"You must be tired," Reggie chuckled. "Otherwise, no way you wouldn't be on your high horse talking about all the stupid things the prosecutor said and did that were appealable, the mistakes the judge made in instructions, all that."

"Well, I mean, if someone were going to appeal, there would be plenty of smoke, if not actual fire. But if the courtroom had not gotten shot up and the main eyewitness hadn't turned out to be, well, I'm not quite sure what, and juror number seven hadn't died, then it . . . yeah, you're right, it sounds ridiculous!"

"So, really, what happened?" Reggie asked.

"You know," Nicki said more seriously, "I really don't know. You know how when you're in the middle of a trial, it just has its own life, and nothing outside of it seems to be in real time? It's like the only thing that's in real time is the trial and everything else that's going on is like going through the motions."

"Yeah, we all know that feeling. Our families too, unfortunately."

"Well, between that feeling that we always have, and all the craziness that was going on, I don't think I ever stopped to consider how unreal that crap was," Nicki said, starting to analyze her experience for the first time. "Things changed so fast. I mean, I know they always do in trial, but things changed so markedly, so fast, it made the changing faster, do you know what I mean? God, I sound like an idiot!

"This is the thing," Nicki went on, after a heavy sigh. "I really don't know what happened. I was there. My client was acquitted. Those sick bastards were convicted. But I don't know, Reggie, there was this whole period in the middle of the trial when the court reporter just stopped typing."

"What do you mean?"

"I mean, the judge was giving instructions to the jury, and the court reporter was not recording it."

"I don't understand."

"The court reporter did not record what the judge was saying," Nicki said a little too loud.

Reggie was quiet for a long time. "Do you think the prosecutor will appeal your client's acquittal?" he finally asked.

"Naaaah. He got all the other defendants. He's not getting any of those witnesses to come back after everything that happened. Nah. I don't think so, why?"

"Let's take a walk," Reggie said, throwing a couple of twenties on the bar and collecting his jacket from the back of his stool.

"Another damn walk?" Nicki said under her breath.

"What?" Reggie asked as he slipped Nicki's jacket around her shoulders. She didn't mean for him to hear her.

"Nothing, nothing."

Washington D.C.'s DuPont Circle was always teeming with activity, day or night. Long known as a LGBTQ-friendly area, the neighborhood often had activity at night that was, well, more interesting. There were small parks where people could hook up, and there was a general feeling of celebration, even when there were no parades going on. A lot of students attending local colleges lived in that area. It was young, fun, and right on the metro. There were great restaurants, a couple of indie bookstores, coffee shops. You could have quiet, tucked away in one of the many townhouses around the area, or you could get lost in a sea of people to meet and things to do.

"DuPont Circle never changes," Reggie said. "When I was here ten years ago, everything looked the same, even some of the faces."

"We got kicked out of a couple of restaurants around here, remember?" Nicki said.

A group of PDSers used to meet periodically for dinner and about every third or fourth time. Trial division attorneys Bernie and/or Mark would create some sort of display that would crescendo into a scene where the manager asked the table to curb its enthusiasm—enough times that a final visit to the table meant paying the check and leaving the uneaten food and half-filled glasses on the table. Ten or twelve drunken lawyers would then spill out of the restaurant into DuPont Circle, where a rousing debate would ensue as to whether the group could finish their dinner somewhere else and be doomed to repeat the display. Usually about half the group decided to press on—the more drunken members—and they stumbled around the area looking for a restaurant that none of them had been ejected from. The other half generally called it a night, swearing that they would embarrass the fallen ones with the tale at some future point, but no one was ever embarrassed, then or later.

"I'm surprised we never got arrested," Reggie laughed. "Some of those nights after we split up got significantly out of hand."

"There were no paparazzi then. Or cellphones that took pictures," Nicki said, not when we all started out, anyway. "Plus, no one gave a shit about us."

"No one gives a shit about us now either," Reggie said, both laughing. "Let's see if there is anything in back. I could use some coffee."

In a back corner of a Starbucks they found a table for two that was a little bit away from the other patrons. The *click, click, click* sound of laptops blended into a weird hum that seemed to purr along with the voices on cell phones. From about every seventh or eighth person, you could also hear music struggling to get out of the headphones that contained it.

Perfect, Reggie thought. *It would be impossible for a human to make out their conversation or any listening device to clearly record it through the RF radiation.*

Reggie moved the foam around the top of his coffee with a stirrer as Nicki blew cool through the whipped cream on top of her hot chocolate.

"What did you think was going on when the court reporter stopped typing the judge's instructions?"

"You know it was so shocking, it took me a few minutes to figure out what was going on. Finally, I did, but after so much had happened, and things had seemingly gone well for my client, I wasn't sure whether to say anything or not. I didn't want to risk a mistrial, but I also didn't want to create such an obvious issue for an appeal by the prosecutor. So, I just sat there. I looked over at the prosecutors and they weren't saying anything either. I just was sort of stuck. So, I stayed stuck and didn't do anything."

"Could you tell if anyone else noticed it besides you and the prosecutor?"

"I don't know. I really do not know. I guess if the jurors noticed, they might not realize the importance of what they were noticing. Nobody said or did anything."

"Do you remember exactly where the judge was in the instructions phase when you noticed the court reporter not typing?" Reggie asked.

"Of course. It was when she was instructing about the appearance of LT. You know, he came back in all banged up. They said he had been in a car accident but with all that had happened, the judge wanted to make sure the jury didn't read anything into it."

"I guess you ordered the transcript already, huh?"

"Yup."

"Well, let's see how it looks when it comes, okay?"

"Reggie, what's going on?"

"The judges panel, which I'm on, as you know, received a complaint about Judge Sullivan's proceedings in the trial," Reggie lied. "I was hoping, mostly for your sake, that there was nothing to the complaint. If the transcript shows her remarks, I'm not so concerned."

"How could they show that?"

"Well, isn't it possible that the court reporter simply recorded that part rather than typing it?"

"Sure, but why would she do that all of a sudden, and not at any other time?"

"Exactly. It does not sound like there was anything particularly critical going on when that happened, so why not? The reporters take short breaks in a long trial because they get hand cramps, right?"

"I guess." Nicki sipped on her hot chocolate and looked out the window onto the circle. It was a particularly busy night, she noticed.

"You good?"

"Just tired." But Nicki was more than tired. Everyone she talked to was not saying something she wanted to know, and her mind was jumping to conclusions and thinking up bizarre conspiracies in one of which she had the judge in cahoots with the Secret Service or LT or both, and the whole trial just a cover for something that didn't have anything to do with F Street at all. Of course, the F Street horror could not have been more real and poor Mrs. Campbell couldn't have been more dead. So, Nicki let herself feel amused at her mind's meanderings but resolved to try to put all the things over which she had no control out of her consciousness, and move on.

"Shall we head back?" Reggie asked. Reggie knew Nicki was having a hard time with everything. He was proud of her, as always, for her fine work in the trial, and he wished he could have done more to ease her mind about everything that had happened. But he could not.

"Sure," Nicki said drawing a last long sip of her hot chocolate and standing. She was looking forward to getting in her bed and sleeping past her alarm and doing nothing the next day but catching up on the news.

As they walked out of the Starbucks and disappeared into the night, Reggie put his arm around Nicki. They walked in silence back to the hotel. Any number of empty cabs passed them by, but Reggie wanted the few extra minutes with Nicki, so he ignored them and waited until they had gotten all the way back to his hotel.

"Do you want me to ride home with you?" Reggie asked as they walked up the brick paved incline to the hotel's entrance.

"Nah, I'm good. Really." Nicki could feel Reggie's worry.

"Okay. Don't forget to stop by the conference tomorrow."

"Yeah, right!" Nicki said laughing. Reggie gave Nicki a bear of a hug—close, tight, engulfing. She held on, longer than usual, enjoying the security and protection of an old and trusted friend. Reggie gave her one last squeeze, and a good-bye pat.

"Talk to you soon. Keep kickin' ass!"

Nicki slid into a cab, gave the driver her address, and leaned her head back on the back of the seat. She was past tired now, and the stress of the trial, all that was still unexplained, had drained her physically and mentally. But she hardly had time to rest her eyes before the cab driver turned on the overhead light as he pulled up to her house.

Home, she thought. *Aaaaaah*. She had told her office when she left it after the trial that she would be in late the next day, maybe not at all.

She walked up the front pathway around to the side of the house where she usually went in. The front door was for guests, she always thought, at least that's how it was when she was growing up, unless you were returning home from a funeral or something like that. She remembered that every time she returned home with her family from a funeral, they went in the front door, as if the seriousness of the occasion warranted the formality of a front door entrance.

Funny, I never thought of that until just this moment.

It amused her, the random thoughts and memories that fill the spaces of a mind too weary to construct coherence or rationality. As the door closed behind her, Nicki felt relieved and in one motion she scooped up the cat in one arm, turned out the lights with the other hand, and headed upstairs. She lay on the bed *for just a sec,* she told herself, but she did not wake up again—still in her clothes—until late the next morning.

The phone pulsed in Reggie's pocket.

"Yo, yo!" Reggie said into his cell phone as he got on the elevator. It was his private phone, not the one he used for work. Only close friends, family, and a few others had that number, and he almost always answered it that way. It was a greeting the guys had started giving each other when they were in college, and all these years later it still just meant a simple, friendly hello with a little macho in it.

"Wassup, bro?"

"Hey, man! How's it hangin'?" Reggie said laughing.

"Just fine, just fine."

"So, how's our girl?"

"She's wiped out, man. Unsettled. But she'll be all right if things stay quiet, I think."

"Good. Thanks, man."

"Anytime, man. Let me know if there is anything else I can do."

"We know where you live."

Reggie and Agent Stackhouse shared a laugh.

Reggie headed up to his room. He had a couple more hours of work to do to for the next day, and he had some follow up calls to make. He was worried about Nicki, though. She was not one to let things go unanswered, he knew from the years when he was with her at PDS. He was concerned that she would poke around quietly and walk right into something that was a danger for her. *Nothing to do about it tonight,* he thought, spreading his papers for the conference out across the bed. As his mind switched gears from the gravity of the last several months to the speech he had to give, Reggie shook his head at the improbability of the twists and turns his life had taken.

CHAPTER TWENTY-FOUR

Your voice makes me tremble inside
And your smile is an invitation
For my imagination to go wild.
—ANONYMOUS

Tommie was wrestling her way out of a fitful dream. She was in that space between fantasy and reality, dream and wakefulness.

"You all right?" David whispered. He was used to Tommie having bad dreams, nightmares even. But he never got comfortable with the feeling of helplessness that her dreaming caused him. His job was to protect the most powerful man in the world. He had done that, successfully, for years under conditions more harrowing than any in history, but he couldn't protect the woman he loved from the dreadful scenes she seemed to have in her head. More lately.

"I had a bad dream."

She always described it that way. Whether it was about deathly creatures chasing her through labyrinths that had no beginning or end, or the loss of something precious and irreplaceable, she simply said, "I had a bad dream." Sometimes she had a dream within a dream within a dream, all of which she struggled to awake from. The nightmares, the dreams that terrified her in her sleep and tormented her when she was awake—sometimes for days, sometimes weeks—often caused her to throw off the sheets as she fought her way out of them. That is what she was doing tonight. Only tonight, she had also been mumbling words. David could not make them out.

"Is there any more water left?"

David rolled over toward the nightstand and handed her the glass of water they kept by the bed.

"You were talking... or something," David said gently.

"I was? What was I saying?"

"I don't know. Do you remember what you were dreaming about?"

"I'm not sure. I was in this place I've never been before, but it was really vivid. It was really tall. I mean it was like the ceiling was a million feet high. And I was sitting in the backseat of a car, I think, or maybe it was an SUV, I don't know. But I remember I kept saying I was thirsty and could I have some water. Then I was someplace else, like in a school or maybe it was a stadium, and I kept running from water fountain to water fountain and none of them worked and I could not get any water. And then I felt woozy, like I was high, except I don't remember ever feeling that kind of lightheadedness before, and my arm really hurt, or my leg, and you were there! But just for a second, and then you were gone. And these people... I don't know."

"What people? Did you know them? What were they doing?"

"I don't know. They weren't nice people; clear faces I've never seen before."

That always disturbed Tommie. The dreams she had where she saw people she had never met and places she had never been would stay with her for days. She didn't understand how a mind could just make up whole people and places it had no reference points for whatsoever. Particularly places. Maybe a troubled or imaginative mind could put parts of faces together and create a new one but the clarity and detail of places she dreamed of freaked her out. When she had a déjà vu, she always wondered if the place or circumstance she felt like she was experiencing for the second time happened first in one of her dreams. But that would mean her dreams were premonitions, and that was a concept she was unwilling to accept. Not with the amount of weirdness, and often terror, in those dreams.

"You don't have to talk about it if you don't want," David said. He could hear in Tommie's voice that she was upset. "Do you want to go back to sleep, can you go back to sleep?"

"I hope so. I'm really tired. I think I was running too fast in my dream," she said laughing quietly, trying to lighten the moment, for herself, for David.

"I'm going to get some more water, want anything else?" David said straightening the tousled bedcovers as he got up.

"No. Thanks, though."

Tommie tried to stay awake at least until David returned. She did not want to fall back to sleep, alone with those images still so vivid in her head. There were plenty of nights when she had fought her way out of a bad dream just to fall back to sleep into the same dream over and over. Sometimes she'd get up, turn on all the lights, turn on the television, and she'd still fall back asleep into the same terrible nightmare.

"You good, now?" David said slipping back into bed, wrapping his body around hers. He held her tight and close for a long time. He wanted to tell her how sorry he was that he couldn't protect her from her nightmares and how bad he felt about her having them so often. But sometimes his words were not as good as his emotions portended and he was afraid it wouldn't come out the way he wanted it. Tommie pulled his arm even tighter around her waist and tucked his hand in hers on his chest. Tommie fell asleep like that, peacefully, but David lay awake a long time thinking before he finally drifted off. When morning came, both were still tired, and neither was ready to get up.

"Things seem to have quieted down at work," Tommie said to David's chest. He was lying flat on his back and Tommie had laid her head on his chest and her arm around his waist.

"I hope so. It's been a difficult few months. We think the press has finally moved on, so that's one good thing. The trial is over, nothing else has blown up or caught on fire for weeks...." They both laughed and began to stir.

"What do you want to do today?"

"Nothing."

"It's a nice day. We could go for a bike ride. Or I could take the boat out if it's not too windy."

David and Tommie were at David's lake house again. He was taking some unusual but much deserved time off and Tommie had snuck away to be with him. It had been a long time since they'd been together at the lake house, much less for four or five days (which they were hoping to get this time).

"The boat. Let's take the boat out," Tommie said. "You want breakfast before we go? I'll make you my world-famous pancakes."

"Yes, let's have your world-famous pancakes, but if I fall asleep at the wheel of the boat and we go veering off course, I'm blaming you when the Coast Guard has to rescue us."

Tommie showered, threw on jeans, and put everything out on the counter. After his shower, David turned on the news to make sure nothing terrible was happening that he needed to be worrying about on his time off, then straightened up around the living room.

"No news is good news," he said, reporting to Tommie.

"Good. Breakfast will be ready in about fifteen minutes. Is that enough time to get the boat ready? If not, why don't you hang out with me in the kitchen?"

"You mean like this?" David laughed as he squeezed her butt cheeks with both hands.

"Not if you want these pancakes."

David hopped up on the counter near the stove where Tommie was cooking and swung his feet back and forth like kids do.

"Can I help?" He had already set the table and put the butter and syrup out.

"Nope, I'm good. What was on the news?"

"Well, one of our disgraced senators is contemplating a comeback, apparently. There was a big pile up on the Beltway, but no one was seriously injured."

"You're right. Nothing new is happening. Good."

It was a nice day. There was a warm, light breeze on the water. The water was calm and there was little traffic on the lake. David drove further out than usual and anchored where he could barely see the shoreline. Tommie lounged in the stern, periodically looking over the side at the schools of fish that were skimming along the top of the water.

"It's so peaceful and quiet. It's nice out here."

"I thought we could both use the quiet. And the calm."

"Okay, now can you tell me more about all that stuff that was going on?" Tommie said sitting up quickly.

"Like what?"

"What do you mean, like what? Like everything! Like, what really happened in that house on U Street? And in Mississippi?"

David had spent longer than usual preparing the boat this time. He checked thoroughly for bugs and bombs and any other devices that could do them harm. He moved the weapon he kept on the boat to a different location because he had always believed that people got tripped up because they followed old habits. He hated lying to Tommie so he didn't. If he couldn't tell her something, he would tell her *that*, but he wouldn't tell her something that was false. This was far too sensitive, and they had been having too nice a time together to jeopardize it, so David tried to make it light.

"You're a nosey little thing."

"Yeah, and?"

"We are *not* going back there," David said. "There isn't much I can tell you, Tommie, except that all of the speculation in the newspapers was way off."

"Well, I know that. You already told me that. Just one little piece of info," Tommie prodded. "One really good nugget."

Tommie knew how responsibly David took his duties and never pried with so much seriousness that would make David feel awkward.

"A juicy nugget? You're such a dork. Here you go ... caramel."

"That was profoundly unfunny," Tommie laughed.

David laughed, but Tommie sensed his discomfort, and she did not want to cast a pall on such a lovely time. Her life wasn't easy either and she needed the time too, to just be. David was glad that Tommie was ok with the levity. He did not want to have to tell her the things he had told Coley about U Street and Mississippi, or what he had told Nicki about the trial and why she was being monitored. Because none of it was true.

Tommie and David stayed on the water until after the sun went down. They ate cheese and crackers, Tommie sipped champagne with strawberries in it, and they talked about the things lovers talk about when they find time alone; friends, family, their love.

"You were coquettish last night," David said as they swayed on the water.

"I think I need a dictionary. It sounds dirty sort of, is it?"

"You know what coquettish means."

"Yes," Tommie admitted, smiling.

"Did I embarrass you?"

"No, well, a little. You know me. I can be … that word … and then very prudish about talking about it."

"I never got that about you."

"I know. Me either. Hey, is there a male version of coquettish?"

"I don't think so," David said, feigning insult.

"I'm going to look it up when we get back to the house."

"What are you going to look up? 'Coquet for boys?'" David teased.

"I'm going to look it up in the dictionary and see what other words are there and see what fits a boy."

"There is no word like that that fits a boy."

"It's French!" Tommie laughed. "Of course, there is a boy version!"

"Ready to head back?"

"Yup, it's getting a little chilly for me."

Tommie cleaned up as David pulled up the anchor, turned the boat towards shore and headed home. It was a smooth ride, and Tommie stood behind David the whole way, arms wrapped around his waist as he drove, her head resting right beneath his shoulder blades. Once in a while David would take both hands off the wheel and grab Tommie's arms, the boat would veer just slightly, and Tommie would squeal "David!"

That night Tommie and David ordered in. They ate Chinese and debated what movie to watch. Tommie wanted to watch something light and fun—*The Princess Bride*. David didn't mind but said you really have to be in the mood for that one, because it was also a little bit silly. So, they compromised on *Men in Black*. Tommie had also tried to get David to watch *The Equalizer* but as much as David liked Denzel, it wasn't light at all and he had to be in the right frame of mind to watch as his girl swooned over another man. So, after reading their fortune cookie fortunes, they locked all the doors, turned down the lights, and settled into *MIB*.

"You're going to fall asleep twenty minutes into the movie," Tommie complained.

"I might."

He often did. There were about eight or ten movies he had only seen half of; it was a habit he had gotten into years before, traveling all over the world with the President when stress, jet lag, and wildly different time zones would keep him from falling asleep, or from staying awake. He would order a first run movie in his hotel room and almost always fall asleep just about halfway in.

"I'm going to poke you when you start drifting."

"Poke to your hearts' content," David smiled as Tommie curled up in his lap on the sofa. But shortly both were asleep, the movie watching them, and neither of them heard the quiet footsteps in the pine needles from the trees in the back of the house.

CHAPTER TWENTY-FIVE

With the F Street trial over, and the U Street lid, things finally quieted down around the White House. President Pierce had been back in the routine of doing the day-to-day stuff that presidents do for weeks now: policy and budget meetings, making deals with legislators, Rose Garden events. He was glad for the lighter schedule, or at least a schedule that did not impose such heavy duties on him. He was also glad for the additional time he was having with Abby. He had decided to do several day trips so that he had more time in D.C., and he was having dinner with Abby almost every night. She was spending more nights there too, and the few residence staff members who knew her enjoyed having her there. She was curious and playful but always polite and respectful. She would sit for hours and watch the chief White House pastry chef form buildings like the Lincoln Memorial, the Capitol, and the White House itself out of flour and cream and sugar and icing. She got to lick the bowl, of course, but never after eight o'clock because that was way too late for an already excited little girl to have so much sugar in her system. Sometimes President Pierce would sneak into the kitchen and watch his daughter conducting grown-up conversations with the head chef over icing, and he would burn those images in his head.

"You know what I would like to see you make one day, Mr. Davidson?" Abby was asking the chef.

"What is that Miss Abby?"

"I would like to see you make a circus!"

"A circus?" Master Chef Davidson.

"Yes! A whole circus! With three rings and of course the elephants must be standing on their hind legs on a stool in one of the tents."

"Tents? Tents too, Miss Abby? That's quite elaborate."

"Well, you certainly cannot have a circus without tents, Roland."

"No, of course you are right, Miss Abby. And for what occasion would we have this circus?"

"Well, a circus, of course! We could have it on the South Lawn. I am quite certain the animals would be pleased to visit the White House."

"And what does the President think of this idea?"

"I have not spoken with him about it yet, but I intend to and I am quite certain he will agree that it is a grand idea."

"Yes, it is a grand idea," the President said stepping into the room. "Abby, when did you come up with this one?"

"Just this moment, Daddy," she laughed.

"Well, it is the grandest of ideas," the President said scooping Abby up and throwing her over his shoulder. "We will talk about it in the morning on the way to school, and I am sure Chef Davidson would be happy to make your circus cake for the grand event."

The President winked at the head chef as he headed toward the tiny elevator to the residence to put Abby to bed. He thought, *there is no human being on this planet I could love more than this child.*

"Daddy?" Abby asked from inside the bundle of covers the President had tucked around her.

"Yes, sweetie."

"Can I come and live with you at the White House?"

"Honey, we've talked about that, right?"

"Yeah."

"And you know how much both me and Aunt Sheila love you, right?"

"Yeah."

"And you know how much Aunt Sheila would miss you if you lived here with me?"

"Yeah."

"So, what is going on, Honey? Did something happen at home? Did you and Aunt Sheila have a fight?'

"No, nothing like that. I was ... well ... I was thinking Aunt Sheila could come and live here, too."

"Sweetheart, sweetheart. You understand that Aunt Sheila and Daddy are not married to each other, right? Did you forget that aunts and daddies don't usually live in the same house?"

"No."

"So, you still understand?"

"Yeah."

This was not the time to correct Abby's grammar, the President thought.

"Are you sure something didn't happen at home?"

I'm sure, Daddy."

"You would tell Daddy, wouldn't you? You know you can tell me anything at all, don't you?"

"Yes, Daddy."

"Why don't you try to get some sleep now? Dream about the circus, and we can talk about it after school tomorrow, ok?"

"Okay, Daddy."

As the President was turning off the light, he heard the tiny voice say, as she was already drifting off ... "Maybe Aunt Sheila can come to the circus."

It broke the President's heart to hear his daughter sound wistful and uncertain like that. He and Abby's mother were diligent and consistent with what they told Abby, and neither of them wanted their situation to hurt her. They knew there would be a time when the explanations they used now would not work anymore; he would not be President Pierce forever, and Abby would soon be around children old enough to question the things parents tell children while they are still young. *Maybe I should call Sheila and check in again.* But he had just talked with her and everything was fine. He did not want to alarm her or make her think he was questioning her parenting.

"David?" President Pierce said into the private phone in the residence. "It's President Pierce."

"Yes, sir," David said.

"I'm a little worried about Abby."

"Is she ill?"

"No, no, nothing like that. She just seemed ... forlorn, tonight, which isn't like her at all, as you know."

"Yes, sir. But maybe she just had a stomachache. Kids sometimes react emotionally to physical ailments, not being able to separate how they feel physically from how they feel emotionally."

David didn't want to sound like he was giving the President a lecture on children; after all he didn't have any children of his own and the President had long been established as an excellent father. But knowing how much the President adored Abby, David also didn't want the President to overreact to something that might have been quite benign. She was a protectee, though, and David had learned everything he could possibly learn from books and from experts about children at all ages and a few months before Abby's birthday, he would get a refresher on what to expect from a girl Abby's age, and with her history.

"I don't think she has a stomachache, David. Out of the blue, she decided we should have a circus on the south lawn, and then she asked about Sheila coming to live in the White House. It isn't the first time, but she hadn't said anything like that for a very long time, and she just seemed, I don't know ... different. More grown-up."

David did not want to point out that Abby was growing up; it wouldn't make the President feel better to have the obvious pointed out to him and, as a parent, he should certainly be ascribed some sort of instinct about his own child.

"Is there something I can do?"

"Yes. I do not want Sheila to think I'm keeping tabs on her; I'm sure she thinks that already, my denials notwithstanding. But would you find out if there is anything going on in her life that Abby may be reacting to?"

"Of course, sir."

"Thank you, David."

"And should we look into logistics for Abby's circus, sir?" David said, the smile in his voice coming through.

"Yes, yes, let's do that," the President chuckled. "Miss Abby will be quite pleased to hear that her secret agent man is working on it. Yes, yes, that's a great idea. In the morning on the way to school, I will tell Abby I called you urgently this evening to look into her circus and that you are getting right on it," the President laughing more easily now.

"Please tell her that if she expects me to bring her a circus, she must learn a new trick."

CHAPTER TWENTY-SIX

Agent Stackhouse already knew what was going on with Sheila. He believed it was his job to know. The President's daughter was an official protectee, and it was the business of the U.S. Secret Service to know about everything and everyone around her. Sheila had been visiting Johns Hopkins. At first, David thought she was visiting a sick friend—maybe a boyfriend she did not want the President or Abby to know about. But Sheila had been getting treatments of some kind. David did not wish to intrude on her privacy further once they figured that out, but now they would need not only to find out what Sheila was getting treated for but also figure out if it was making her sick enough for Abby to know something was wrong.

David did not want to use the resources of the agency for this. He had top men and women he trusted with the life of the President, of course, but he had a gut instinct that this was one to call in a favor for personally.

"Good evening," David said reaching out his hand as he walked through the front entrance. "I am very sorry to disturb you so late in the evening."

"I never mind you calling on me, Agent Stackhouse. I know you only reach out to me when it is of a most critical nature."

"I appreciate that. We . . . appreciate that."

"Would you like something to drink?"

"No, ma'am. But please go ahead."

"Why don't you get right to it, Agent Stackhouse."

"Of course, of course. We need to get the medical records of an individual currently being treated at Johns Hopkins. The information we need is very limited and discreet."

"Sounds a little different than the last matter we dealt with."

"It is. It is of a more personal matter for President Pierce."

David did not want to give the impression that there was something wrong with the President; everyone knows the President of the United States is cared for by doctors at Walter Reed National Military Medical Center. Something at Johns Hopkins would signal something undisclosed. But he would rather arouse speculation about President Pierce than reveal the real situation.

"I trust President Pierce is in good health."

"Absolutely, yes, ma'am. It is related to a close, family..."

"No need to explain," she interrupted.

"Thank you, ma'am." David was relieved. The less he had to lie the better for everyone, including her. Especially her.

"I'll have the warrant ready in the morning, Agent Stackhouse," she said as she escorted David to the foyer.

"Thank you, Judge. I will make sure the President knows about your assistance."

"No need, Agent Stackhouse."

David knew that she meant that. Not as a mechanism for keeping her fingerprints off sticky matters, but because her own work ethic required the utmost prudence and discretion.

"Get some rest, Judge Sullivan. Again, I am sorry to have disturbed you so late."

The next day, it only took an hour for Agent Stackhouse to get access to Sheila Cooper's records after picking up the warrant. He did not see Judge Sullivan when he picked it up; she had just left a confidential envelope for him with her housekeeper, and she had called in a favor from a judge friend of hers in Maryland, where Johns Hopkins is located. Neither of them wished for protocols to differ from normal protocols. Now, David was sitting in a small, window-less but well-lit room off the records wing. He had been there more times than he wanted to remember, and there was little chance the information he would find in the pages in front of him now would reveal any better information than in the past. It was always harder with people you knew and liked.

A clerk arrived with a thick file, identified himself, offered a few pleasantries and asked David for his credentials, which David provided. The clerk took note of the badge and picture, checked the picture against David's face. David looked older, the clerk thought; worry-older. The clerk kept that to himself and motioned to David to take a seat at the foot of the small conference-style table. The clerk offered David coffee or coke; David opted for the coke. The clerk nodded his agreement. "Good choice. Hospital coffee. I'll be right back," he said, handing David the file.

David settled into the chair and waited. He was anxious but he did not want to risk the clerk seeing something he wasn't supposed to or, more importantly, making connections he shouldn't make.

More moments passed than David would have liked. He scrolled through the texts he had received on his way to Johns Hopkins and while he was winding his way through the hospital hallways. *Good,* he thought, *nothing urgent.*

"I'm so sorry, Agent Stackhouse," the clerk said as he rushed through the threshold of the doorway. "Got waylaid on my way back here. Here you are," he said, handing David a cold Coke wrapped in a white paper towel.

"No problem at all. Thank you. Shall I call or text you when I'm finished?"

"Sure, that's fine if it's in the next hour or less. I'm off soon."

"Got it. I won't be any longer than that," David said. He did not want to have to interact with any more people that he needed to.

The clerk nodded and backed out of the office, pulling the door close.

David took a deep breath, opened the file, and scanned to the inside of the jacket by date, backwards to forward. He took out a pen and small notepad, jotting down abbreviations that he did not have time to work through now, and other words, tests, actions, dates that he thought were important.

It was worse than he expected. David had speculated that Sheila might have breast cancer. It had been his experience that some women preferred to deal with breast cancer privately. Others, he knew, were buoyed by the help of family, breast cancer support groups and the like, and he was glad the disease was no longer something that just was not talked about. Sheila, he figured, would be glad others had the kind of support that is now available but would seek to deal with hers privately and discreetly, not even telling family and close friends, likely. But it was worse than that.

"Ductal adenocarcinoma" he read. "Unresectable. Locally advanced."

Shit. I should have known. The Sol Goldman Pancreatic Cancer Research Center at Hopkins is world renowned. Shit!

The file was thick with information about tests and experimental trials and scans that looked worse and worse. He did not need to read through all that now. What would be the point? He has read the word "terminal" enough times.

He texted the clerk, who returned more quickly than he had from the soda run. He did not know him, but to the clerk, David looked even older now. But he was used to that.

David thanked the clerk, asked where he could dispose of the coke can, and headed back down the all too familiar hallways. He stuffed the paper towel in his pants pocket.

On the drive back to D.C., Agent Stackhouse's mind raced between incongruence, irreconcilability, sadness. Sheila was dying of terminal pancreatic cancer. She deserved her privacy, and the death she preferred, whatever that was, but she was the mother of the President's child. Of course, hardly anyone knew that, really. Not even Abby. Still, the President had asked him to find out if something was going on in her life, and either way, he would find out eventually. And poor Abby. She adored her "aunt." And what would be the President's plan for her care going forward?

There were places along the Baltimore-Washington Parkway, near NSA, and also near the Secret Service's training facility at Beltsville, where cell phones went dead for several seconds. David timed his departure from the hospital so that he would hit both of those areas on the return to D.C. He was not ready to talk to the President. And this was not a phone conversation anyway. It was an in the residence face-to-face, and he was in no hurry to have it.

David's mind raced.

Maybe I should talk to Sheila first. No, no, that would make it worse. Maybe I can convince the President to let Sheila come to him in her own time and her own way. No, he'll never buy that. He'll tell me he agrees, and then he'll try to sneak out and go see her.

The records showed that Sheila's diagnosis was recent and that there had not been time for a second opinion yet. That was one thing he could tell the President. Sheila would be furious, though, at someone else revealing her secret. No doubt she had already thought of the exact time it would be right, and fair, to tell the President, and there was nothing in her life that would make her think that information was not hers to communicate.

"Shit! Shit! Shit!" David said out loud, banging his fists on the steering wheel. And then it hit him. Just like that. He had the answer to the whole terrible, terrible situation.

That is what the craziness and secrecy of U Street and Mississippi was all about anyway.

CHAPTER TWENTY-SEVEN

"The means we use must be as pure as the ends we seek."
—DR. MARTIN LUTHER KING, JR.

"Everyone is here," Agent Stackhouse said. Seconds later, the President met Agent Stackhouse in front of a wall in a corridor near the Map Room—the wall with the giant Civil War oil painting on it. David pressed something in his pocket, the wall disappeared, picture and all, and they stepped through, leaving no observable sign of where they had just been or where they were going.

Highly scrutinized and carefully cropped images of the briefing room in the basement of the White House had been released to the public by the President last year during a national emergency. The White House wanted to show the world that the President and all his top military aides were alive, well, and together as they planned for the nation's protection and response. But all the photo revealed was a bunch of military and national security aides sitting around a conference table in a wood-paneled room talking to a giant TV screen which showed the President in some "undisclosed location." Only about thirty people on the planet, still living, had the remotest idea where that room under the White House was, what else was there, or even how you got down there. Indeed, most of the people who had been there could not tell you how they got in or how they got out. Fewer than that ever knew where the President was when he was in an "undisclosed location," though any number of people would swear they did.

That almost none of the people who visited the President's underground bunker could tell you how they got down there was doubly true for this meeting. Except for David, and the President of course, none of the meeting's other participants could have told anyone how to get back there. Once or twice in presidential history that fact precipitated exceedingly unhappy consequences. At least one U.S. counter-intelligence agent was tortured to death when he failed to reveal the entrance to the bunker. Though he would have, as the stories about his loyalty went, he had not actually sacrificed his life in execution of duty. He really had not known.

"Gentlemen," the President said entering the room from a different door from the one everyone else had used, "don't get up. Thank you for coming."

"Good morning, sir."

"Morning, Mr. President."

"Hello, Mr. President."

"Shall we get started?"

David took a seat at the table one chair away from the President, to his left. Homeland Security Secretary Brown was to the right of the President, Detective Tyler was catty-corner across the table towards the middle, Reggie Stone was on the end. A couple of high-level NASA and NIH officials were present as well.

"Gentlemen," the President began, "first let me thank all of you personally for your contributions to the difficult missions we have completed recently, and the complex work we have conducted over the last few years. You have discharged your duties with great care and commitment. Your involvement has, for each of you, required significant sacrifice. Your service will be rewarded.

"We have achieved something that is staggering. *Staggering*. Staggering in its breadth, depth, scope, proportion, and completeness. Gentlemen, we, the United States of America, have changed the world. Not just now, in real time, but forever. Fully, thoroughly, and comprehensively. There is no discovery, by any nation, at any time in this world's history, that approximates what we have done here. What your service has helped us do. There will be none to equal it in the future.

"Second, including the doctors and scientists, and now you, I can count on my hands the number of people who are being trusted with this information at this time. I know that you have been briefed on the level of secrecy this intelligence requires. Some of you have undergone rigorous investigation so that your clearance level could be raised appropriately. Sorry for that."

"You need to understand, truly understand, what all of this means. Men, women and, God-bless us, some children lost their lives so that this project could live. More than we expected. More than we feared. That is a dreadful reality which we will . . . I will have to live and die with. For some the end never justifies the means. That juxtaposition will be something you individually will have to wrestle with.

"It won't be easy. As much as some of you have seen and experienced, this may well be the most difficult thing you contemplate your entire lives. These are the things that measure a man, or woman. There is no doubt this will be, in the end, the only measure of me."

The room had filled with tension. While it was clear that the President was getting ready to impart something that he felt very strongly about, something monumentally beneficial for the world, there were also unanswerable questions of right and wrong, good and bad, weighing on him.

"Colleagues," the President continued, "we, the United States of America, have discovered . . ."

Just then, a cell phone rang out, loudly, lengthily.

"I'm so sorry, Mr. President. Please pardon the disruption. We had a situation in my office earlier this morning, and it was significant enough for an emergency update." The Homeland Security Secretary spoke gravely as he stood, moved back towards the door, and whispered into the phone.

"Yes, yes, I see. Are we sure? Do we have a plan? When will we have one? Does anyone know what the demands are?" Secretary Brown said.

He had the attention of everyone in the room now. The disquiet created by hearing his side of the conversation left everyone, including the President, distracted and engaged.

"Is everything all right?" the President asked. The room was after-a-snowstorm still.

"Robert?" the President asked impatiently.

"Mr. President, my chief of staff Thomasina Coles, is missing. When she didn't make it in to work this morning, we knew something was wrong but we, obviously, hoped we were wrong. FBI agents have just confirmed that it appears to be a kidnapping."

"A kidnapping?" the President said, jumping to his feet. "Are you sure?"

"Yes, Mr. President, we are sure," Secretary Brown said. "It appears that there was some sort of struggle at her home. She is missing; her briefcase is missing but none of her valuables. And there was a note. It said, 'you will hear from us,' in block letters cut out from newspapers and magazines. They're testing for prints now, but we don't expect to find any."

Agent Stackhouse had not heard much after the word "missing." His mind sped to the last time he had spoken with Tommie—just the night before—how she sounded, what she said, what was going on at work for her that day, what she had been working on that might have been sensitive. The President's voice jolted Agent Stackhouse from his thoughts and now he was on his feet too, making calls on two different phones, checking the White House tracker, trying to find out what the hell was going on.

Now, the President's secret, underground containment was buzzing with new business, and the critical information he had called the meeting to impart remained in the President's head. The same set of people, though, who were together to hear the President's announcement, remained together, though they moved upstairs to the situation room where the secretary to the cabinet and the head of Joint Operations Command joined them.

The President spoke directly and decisively, "Agent Simmons, who has been to Ms. Coles' home and confirmed that this is indeed a kidnapping, will address you shortly with details. But I wanted to share my thoughts on this.

"First, many of you know Thomasina Coles, the Homeland Security Secretary's chief of staff. Some of you do not. For those of you who do not, I consider her a friend. She is Secretary Brown's friend. She is extraordinarily competent and has been an exceedingly loyal friend to this administration and this president. And I am sure I don't have to tell you the intelligence and security importance of the Homeland Security's chief of staff being taken. Her speedy and safe return is the number one priority of my administration right now.

"Second, from the intelligence side, we don't know why Ms. Coles was taken. But she has held some codes, she does maintain a top-secret clearance, and she has held other clearances as required. We could be dealing with something official, something top secret, something personal, or just some nut. Right now, we don't know. Because of some of the administration's priorities that she has been exposed to and/or has had access to, we are of course worried about what condition we might find her in. Time is critical. Find her."

President Pierce was one of the lucky ones. Sure, he'd done a spectacular job when he picked his cabinet and senior officials, avoiding many of the mistakes most presidents make early on. He had had very few fights with or hold-ups by the Senate committees responsible for confirming key appointees, no one had to withdraw due to scandal unearthed in the vetting process, and they worked well together from the beginning. He made sure not to mete out favorite treatment for loyalty; everyone's loyalty was expected, and everyone got to ride on the plane when it was their turn. So, he was comfortable relying on their dedication and discretion, and he couldn't imagine having to be in a bunker with better men and women.

Still, all of this was a lot to ask, he knew. He was about to share with them the greatest discovery known to man, including the difficult choices that had to be made to get there, the consequences of those choices, and now he was asking them to put everything on hold for someone many of them didn't even know.

"Before we adjourn for what I hope will be a truly short period, let me say again what your commitment has meant to me and what your continued discretion will mean for the country. We'll see each other soon."

CHAPTER TWENTY-EIGHT

It didn't work. The President's attempt to control the message did not satisfy almost anyone, and members of the President's cabinet convened informally upstairs in the Roosevelt Room. It was smaller and less centrally located than the Cabinet Room where they met monthly with the President, and it was further away from the Oval Office. It also wouldn't likely raise any concerns with the president—they were in the building anyway.

"What do we know about what's happening?" the NASA director asked.

National Institutes of Health head Baker offered, "it appears that each of us has only a piece, or pieces, of the puzzle. But that together...."

"But none of us is authorized to share our respective pieces," the energy secretary interrupted. I suggest we do what the President asked us to. Keep our powder dry until he gets this other situation under control."

"I agree," the NASA head said. "I don't like it, but I agree."

There was less than unanimity in the sentiment—several officials demonstrated it in their body language—but there was accord in the outcome. They would return to the business of their respective agencies, provide whatever support they could to the President in his newest challenge, and wait.

"David. David? Agent Stackhouse!" David heard the President's voice through the fog of what he had just learned.

"Yes! Yes, sir. Yes, Mr. President?"

"David, join me in my dining room for a bit of lunch. I'd like to talk to you."

The President had finished giving instructions to other staff and was preparing to leave the Situation Room.

"Sir..."

"Now, Agent Stackhouse."

The President did not enjoy having to talk to David that way. He disliked having to talk to anyone that way. Lunch for two was already set up in the President's small dining room near the Oval Office. *The President had already arranged their meeting*, Agent Stackhouse thought as he followed him back towards the Oval Office from the Situation Room. *Maybe just as well.*

His head was spinning. He should be out looking for his girl, though he had already talked to a half dozen of his agents, Chief Coley, and a couple of his intelligence agency friends. They were way down the road on their plan to find Tommie.

But Agent Stackhouse still felt trapped. His sworn oath and obligation were to the President of the United States and his family. His position did not permit him to be distracted by other matters or otherwise engaged in activity not directly related to the President's safety. His code, his sense of duty and honor, "Worthy of Trust and Confidence"—the U.S. Secret Service's motto—was overwhelming. And for the first time, the very code Agent Stackhouse lived by was in the line of his own fire.

"Have a seat, David," the President said as they settled into the dining room.

The President's waitstaff had been told not to disturb the President once he was seated, so they served everything except dessert and waited for the bell to ring in the tiny kitchen where they remained nearby.

Agent Stackhouse was not hungry. The President knew that, and it was not his place to tell a grown man he should eat, especially one whose job it was to take a bullet for him. Agent Stackhouse certainly could take care of himself.

"I know you don't feel like eating, David. But you should. That is all I'm going to say about it. I'm not your father."

The President thought using psychology might help so he chomped down on his turkey sandwich and pretended to have too full a mouth to talk. It worked. Agent Stackhouse did not feel like initiating a conversation and small talk was out of the question, so he filled the silence by eating his own sandwich.

When they were both nearly finished, the President said, "David, go get your girl."

"Sir?"

"Go get her."

"Sir, with all due respect, I'm not sure what you're saying. And my duties are..."

David did not want to insult the President by playing dumb at this moment. *Does he know about my relationship with Tommie? Or is he using the words "your girl" loosely? Certainly, he knows we are close colleagues,* David thought.

"I know what your duties are, Agent Stackhouse. For once in your damn life, break a rule, and go get our Tommie."

"Mr. President..."

"Let me put it this way Agent Stackhouse. Ms. Coles is an integral part of this administration generally, and the Office of the President specifically. I want her found, and there is no one better—or with more incentive—than you."

"But..."

David did not know how much to protest the order or the implication. He was going to find her, in or outside of the law. That was not really a question for him. But if the President knew about their relationship, and the outside of the law manner prevailed, he would be exposing the President to charges of unlawful actions and, no doubt, investigations.

"Dammit, David! You are wasting time none of us has, especially Tommie. Call your friends. I'll make sure your team has any information the official group develops. I know I do not really have to convince you, David. I know you were going to do it anyway. So, go ahead. You have my blessing. Your involvement will also obviate the need for me to deal with the Gang of Eight, or create a Presidential Finding, or any of that."

The Gang of Eight had not even occurred to David. He knew that President Pierce—like all presidents had conferred upon him—the ability to plan for, conduct, and support secret missions with congressionally appropriated funds, without providing the public, or even most of the Congress, any information about them. David had not seen or heard about it being operationalized very often in his tenure with the USSS but maybe he wouldn't. Still, David certainly knew personally those eight leaders of the congress who had that power—and he was figuratively smacking himself for not thinking of it.

"And," the President continued, "you know the government's policy regarding negotiating with terrorists. If we learn Tommie is being held by terrorists . . . well, you know as well as I how that might turn out."

"Yes, sir," Agent Stackhouse said, rising from the table.

It did not make sense to David to continue to argue with the President. Nor did it matter right now whether the President knew he had a personal relationship with Tommie.

Maybe he was counting on it, David thought.

But it didn't matter. He was the boss. And David *was* going to do it anyway.

"Be careful."

"Yes, sir. Thank you. For . . . lunch."

Later, the President told a limited number of his closest advisors that

Agent Stackhouse would be reachable only through him for the next several days. To a person, they protested the president's close involvement in this, and the viability of his being the contact for his own agent. But the President knew if he told his advisors that David was working on something personal for him, they would not inquire further, and they didn't.

But they also didn't believe him. They knew the President had likely asked Agent Stackhouse to help with Tommie Coles' rescue mission. They just didn't know why.

CHAPTER TWENTY-NINE

Agent Stackhouse was on the phone again as soon as he left the West Wing.

"Stone," Reggie Stone answered.

"Reggie? David. You still in the building?"

"Yes. Stopped by the Mess for a quick sandwich."

"Don't go anywhere. I'll be there in two minutes."

The White House Mess was small and usually crowded, but not yet, and David found Reggie sitting in a table for two along the far wall—away from the serving area. He was in a dark suit and tie, and with his visitor access pass hanging around his neck, he looked exactly like anyone else moving about the grounds. That was good, David knew. David ordered a large coffee in a to-go cup and sat briefly. Reggie did not like the way his old friend looked.

"I have to ask you," Reggie said. "What the hell was the President getting ready to say when all hell broke loose? I mean, that was some build up and speech he was giving."

David had no interest in talking about that, but he needed help with finding Tommie, minutes mattered, and Reggie was a friend.

"I gotta put that on the backburner right now, Reg. You deserve to know, obviously, the President was seconds away from telling you all. But there's a shift right now and it's finding Tommie."

David would have preferred to have said "Homeland Security Secretary's chief of staff Thomasina Coley"—he preferred not to be so informal given the circumstances—but they were already whispering as it was. The Mess was not crowded but there were still ears around.

"I know that Stack, I was in the room when it happened." Reggie didn't want to argue with his friend though. He looked like shit.

"Who are the best snatch-n-grab guys that you know of?

"In or out?" Reggie said.

"Both."

"The best guys 'in' are Fifth Special Ops out of Joint Special Operations Command. The best guys 'out' are out of Miami. Their rep is mixed, though."

"What do you mean?"

"They've never failed, but their tactics are, well.... they've done some nasty stuff, even for special ops. You wouldn't want your hands in it."

"And the guys in the Fifth?"

"They are very good. But they could be anywhere right now—they could be downrange. I'd have to make some calls."

"Make some calls for me, would you? And give me a number for the guys in Miami."

CHAPTER THIRTY

The next couple of hours for Agent Stackhouse were a whirlwind of phone calls, IOUs, tactics, and weapons. David called in many of his chits, and he bought a cache of high-powered weaponry and explosives with his own money. He had made a lot of friends over the years, helped a lot of people, so no one accepted his IOUs—they just asked, "what can I do?"

In extraordinarily little time, David had engaged the group in Miami, learned the most probable of the kidnapping scenarios, and had three tactical plans laid out with land, air, and amphibian support from friends in the Black Ops community, Marine Recon, Delta, and Seal Team operators. Most of the guys, and one woman, were retired military. But not all.

David was careful in his engagement with the Miami guys. He trusted Reggie and took him at his word when he told David that he should not have his hands in it with them. When he was ready to pull the trigger, he sent his friend to the food court on K Street to set it up.

Reggie arrived at K Street around noon, almost 24 hours after the news of Tommie's kidnapping had shaken David to his core. It was the height of the lunch hour. The food court was teeming with people who worked in the area and ate there regularly. It was busy, and noisy, and the smells from the Greek place competed with those from Five Guys, the Pizzeria, Au Bon Pain, and the Jamaican restaurant. Amid all the clatter and the bustle of hungry government workers on short breaks in long lines, and others from the law and lobbying firms also in the building, there were always four or five chess matches going on there. It was an odd sight. But when regular players paired together, a small crowd would stand around them and watch their moves. Part of the sport in playing amidst so much distraction, disruption, and disarray was maintaining concentration in the middle of so much chaos. Only the elite players met regularly there.

Reggie stood by the big glass doors that led to the building's rear elevators and parking garage. He watched the table closest to the doors, to the left, against the wall. He was right on time. The game looked like it would wrap up any minute.

"Checkmate," the man with his back to the wall said.

"Fine game," his opponent said rising. And, as smoothly and quickly as the loser stood, Reggie was seated across from the winner. Reggie nodded his greeting, the winner barely looked up from the board, and they began their play in silence.

Reggie was white. His moves went quickly. King's pawn forward two squares. When his opponent moved *his* King's pawn forward two squares, the famous four-move checkmate began. Reggie moved his King's bishop to attack his opponent's King's Bishop's pawn. Reggie then placed his Queen in a position to attack King's Bishop's pawn. Right before Reggie took his opponent's King's Bishop's Pawn with the Queen, he said "checkmate is upon us, my good friend."

"Indeed," said his opponent. "You are adept at the four-move checkmate."

"I have time for another round," Reggie said.

"I believe there are others waiting, but perhaps we will meet again. My table is number 8-77."

"Thank you, friend," Reggie said rising. And he was gone. With the code. The next player sat down across from the loser, this time, instead of the winner.

CHAPTER THIRTY-ONE

"Judge of your natural character by what you do in your dreams."
—RALPH WALDO EMERSON

Tommie fell in and out of consciousness, having flash-back-like dreams. In her mind, she was back in Oklahoma City working at the bomb site with Fairfax County and Miami Dade search and rescue after Timothy McVeigh blew up the Alfred P. Murrah Federal Building.

All those little babies, Tommie thought through the drug-induced dimness of her mind.

They were floating now, all those little babies, like angels, except that in the muddle of Tommie's assaulted psyche, those angelic babies were covered with concrete and wires and debris that stabbed into their little hands and tore open their little chests.

Then Tommie was in Nevis, West Indies taking in the beauty of its unspoiled land, feeling the warmth of its recuperative sea air, enjoying the challenge of climbing Nevis peak with her guide, Lynnell, in Hardtimes Gingerland.

In the White House now, stumbling over the first words she ever spoke in the Oval Office.

Back in Oklahoma City, incidentally coming upon the letterhead of her own agency in the wreckage, and the hand of an ATF agent sticking out of the ruins—the last federal agent to be recovered from the bomb site. She did not know him, or anyone else who knew him, but she had been moved by the experience in a way she couldn't explain and when his funeral was scheduled on her birthday, she thought fate was directing her to go back to Oklahoma City for the funeral of a man she did not know. So she did.

Now Tommie was sitting cross-legged in front of the old phonograph in the dining room in her mother and father's house.

"Well, I don't know what will happen now. We've got some difficult days ahead. But it doesn't matter with me now. Because I've been to the mountaintop. And I don't mind. Like anybody, I would like to live a long life. Longevity has its place. But I'm not concerned about that now. I just want to do God's will. And He's allowed me to go up to the mountain. And I've looked over. And I've seen the promised land. I may not get there with you. But I want you to know tonight, that we, as a people, will get to the promised land. And I'm happy, tonight. I'm not worried about anything. I'm not fearing any man. Mine eyes have seen the glory of the coming of the Lord."

Tommie was listening to an album of Martin Luther King's speeches. Over and over, she played *I've Been to the Mountain Top* and cried. Over and over, she played *I Have A Dream* and was lifted up. When Dr. King was assassinated, Tommie played the "Dream" speech until she almost wore out the grooves, but she could recite it by heart.

Now she was in Syria.

Now she was nine years old, dancing with her father, her little stocking feet balancing on her father's shoes as he led her around like a princess.

In between the randomness of her mind's chaos, when Tommie had fleeting moments of clarity, she tried to memorize the tonality and pitch of the voices she heard.

"Is everything in place?"

"Yes."

"Any intel on movements from the White House?"

"Our man at Homeland says things are very buttoned up but believes they are running the typical operation out of the Situation Room."

"His cover is still holding?"

"Yes."

"He still has good access?'"

"Yes."

"If anything changes, I want to know immediately. Otherwise, we're dark for the next two days."

"Yes, sir."

"And get that damn woman some food and water before the sodium pentothal fries her brain."

"Will do."

Tommie heard mostly what sounded like a man's voice whispering between hiccups, but she had a good ear, an ear trained for intonation pattern, and she tried as hard as she could to memorize contour and timbre.

Then, she was at the lake house with David, giggling about pasghetti.

"You're amok," she heard David say, and then she blacked out.

CHAPTER THIRTY-TWO

Joe Peirinase was sitting on his deck drinking a beer and watching a game when he saw David come around the side of the house. Joe had kept the house in the Maryland country that he had moved to after his wife was killed. He could not bear to stay in the home they had shared, and he looked for something as different, and far away as he could get from the memories of her. He pulled himself out of his lounge chair and met David halfway down the stairs.

"Good to see you, man," Joe said, extending his hand, then leaning his shoulder in for the buddy hug. "Coley said you might come by. I'm sorry to hear about Ms. Coles. Any word?"

"We have a good source," David said following Joe back up the stairs to the deck. "We're working on him now. We're almost there but he has been ambitious about his ability to handle some of the tactics. He's only hanging on by the skin of his teeth now. We hope we can get the last piece of information we need before he stops coming back to consciousness altogether. We think Tommie's still alive. But we don't have much time," David said stumbling on the landing as he heard himself. *Still alive.*

"Careful, man," Joe said as David's legs appeared to buckle underneath him. He had faltered physically upon the implication of his language. His body could not handle the torment of his mind.

"I'm all right, man. Bad knee," David lied. "Look, we need one more man."

"Who you got?"

"The boys out of Miami. Some specials ops. Some retired."

"David, those Miami boys . . ."

"I know, Joe. I know. But there's nothing those crazy ass guys could do that I wouldn't abide. They took my girl, Joe, right under my goddamned nose. I have to find her, and they have to pay. And in the end, in *their* end, there won't be any doubt about how painfully those assholes met their maker."

"Your girl? I didn't . . . when . . . does Coley . . . ."

"Are you in or not, man? If we get what we need before this sucker croaks, we're dark for the rest of the day, and on the move tonight," David said.

David had slipped when he said "my girl," Joe knew that. He didn't have any judgment. "Yeah, of course."

"Thank you, Joe."

"You'd do it for me, man. I know that."

"I would."

"Do you have time for a beer?" Joe asked. David looked like shit to Joe too and he wanted to give him five or ten minutes of downtime, of rest, before they moved on to tougher endeavors.

David thought about it for a moment. It was tempting. But time was short, and he needed every faculty and part of him needed to stay in warrior mode.

"Thanks, I better not, Joe."

"Understood."

"All right so at midnight and ten tonight, pull into the Amoco station off 50 West right before the parkway. Pump number seven. The attendant won't have time to clear the sale right before you. At exactly 12:10, the amount of the sale on the pump will be your coordinates. You will then have twenty-seven minutes to meet us. We will have fourteen minutes to get in and get Tommie out before the place blows. The fire department will be called from an untraceable cell. We will all need to be gone before the fire department turns onto the street off 295 North. Then we are dark again on this. Permanently."

"All right. David?" Joe called as David took the stairs back down three at a time.

"Yeah, man?" David said, without turning around.

"Fourteen minutes may not give you enough time to acquaint those assholes with their Lord," Joe said.

Joe was worried about David's objectivity. He had been in enough dogfights to know that perspective is everything and that mistakes, fatal mistakes, happen when a man's mind meanders from the mission. Missions are black and white. There is no room for softness, no time for debate. Everybody's life depends on everyone else bringing their A game, completing their tasks. In mission, there is no family, no wife, no child, no love, no desire. There is only precision. And completion. Joe had learned that the easy way, and the hard way.

"I got this," David said, his temperature rising.

He knew damn well he had to get his feelings out of the way. He didn't need anybody telling him that. And he would. The life of close friends and colleagues depended on that. Tommie's life was defined by it. Also, if something happened to him, the President might not learn about Sheila's cancer in time to save her. And he would have lost one of the best women he had ever known, and Abby would have lost her mother.

"All right, man" Joe said, sensing David's indignation. "Assets?"

"Yours are in a black duffel bag under your deck," David answered.

"Do we have any air?" Joe asked, walking down the steps after David. He didn't want his voice to carry.

"Yes."

David had friends all over the military and CIA. And he knew choppers. He could tell out-of-sight and miles away whether a helicopter was an Apache, a Stallion, a Chinook, a Bell, a Huey, a Black Hawk. He could tell Russian from Israeli, Saudi from Chinese. Just from the sound. They all sounded like thunder, even from a distance, no thunder roared the same, and David could always tell just which storm was coming.

"Where are we?" David said into his cell phone as he got in the car.

"We're green," the voice on the other end of the line said.

"How was the Curtis Mayfield show?" David asked.

"Freddie's Dead."

"Too bad," David said. "I was hoping the show would draw a bigger crowd."

"Way these things go sometimes."

"Yeah."

David had been talking to Coley in code.

"The Miami boys got the intel we needed," Coley told David, "but the source... well... you know what Ecclesiastes says, 'for everything there is a season, and a time for every matter under heaven: a time to be born—'"

"And a time to die," David finished.

CHAPTER THIRTY-THREE

"Hold on, I'm comin'."
—SAM & DAVE

David was tired. He had had just enough time to nap, shower, and get to the Amoco station before Joe arrived at 12:10 to fill-up at pump number seven. It was now 11:02, exactly 48 hours from when he heard the words that took the breath from his body: "My agents have just confirmed. It appears that she was kidnapped."

David could not get the Homeland Security Secretary's words out of his head. He knew that what the President predicted if Tommie's captors were terrorists was dead-on: the government would not negotiate with them. And Tommie would die. Like any covert snatch-n-grab, Tommie's rescue had to be executed with keen calculation and uncommon flawlessness.

David started thinking of Tommie as Ms. Thomasina Coles, chief of staff to the Secretary of the Department of Homeland Security. He tried to think about her as officially as he could. He made himself forget she was the love of his life. He made himself forget how her tight, athletic body felt against his. He made himself forget the first time they made love. The last time they made love. He made himself forget her smile, the smell of her hair, the sweetness of her voice. He thought about the mission, about securing the package. But his need to ensure that the idea of anyone visiting harm upon Tommie would be demonstrably contrary to reason—for any reason, at any time, at any price—took him to the darkest place he had ever been in his life. He thought way too long, and thoroughly, about how he would break their knees, then dislocate their fingers, then crush their balls, all in that order, then jam one of them down their throat, and the other one up their ass. And then he thought about resigning.

What we think, we become, David thought, remembering the old Buddhist proverb. But in his head, all he heard was Sam and Dave: "Hold on . . . I'm coming."

At five minutes to midnight, David's private cell rang. Only two people had that number, Tommie and the President. He was praying that it was Tommie but then it occurred to him that if Tommie was calling, she probably had a gun pointed at her head.

"Stackhouse," David answered.

"David?"

"Yes, Mr. President."

"I hear the Miami boys are in town."

"I heard that too, sir."

"Your hands are clean?"

"Of course, Mr. President."

"Are we close?"

"Very close, sir."

"Hurry up," the President said.

"Yes, sir," David said, but the President was already gone. David's mind was so busy with his mission, but it struck him how urgent the President sounded.

David's crew was way ahead of the White House's official rescue mission. The White House was just confirming a possible motive *and* a possible location; David's team already knew where Tommie was. They did not care why. Still, David was glad to learn that both the official and the covert efforts had led to the same place. That increased the chances of the intelligence being accurate. That also meant his crew was working well together, something that was always a challenge for some of the special ops guys. They tended to man all the way up—all of them—David knew, and while the mission was always the only priority, secretly they all wanted to be the hero. Why shouldn't they?

At 12:05, David pulled into the Amoco station. Someone was at pump number seven. He hoped they didn't take too much longer and kicked himself for not getting there just two or three minutes earlier, but he didn't want to draw attention to himself by lingering too long at the gas station. David pulled up behind the driver pumping gas and decided to get out.

"Nice night," he said to the stranger, leaning against his car.

"Yeah. They said rain though," the stranger said making small talk.

David was hoping the driver would feel uncomfortable with a man he didn't know walking up on him and talking to him out of the blue, and would then hurry up, which he did. The man released the catch that automatically delivers gas into the tank and manually pressed the lever as far back as it would go. The pump sped up and the stranger finished, paid with a credit card, and quickly drove away, not even waiting for his receipt. David cleared the sale, tore up the man's receipt in tiny little pieces and threw them away in two different trash cans. David pumped exactly $19.68. He pretended to wash the windows with the wiper that stays in the solution near the gas pump, caught the outline of Joe's car in his sideview mirror coming up 295N, got in his car, and left.

Joe pulled up at exactly 12:10. He noted the numbers on pump seven—$19.69—cleared the sale, pumped $5.00 in to ensure the prior sale was gone, entered the numbers $19.69 on the neighborhood grid he had a copy of, and took off toward Route 50. Neither David nor Joe knew that when David drove off, the sale on pump seven rolled up one cent from

$19.68 to $19.69. All the pumps did that there. The owners had found a way to round up every sale one penny, an amount they figured no one would notice, and they pocketed hundreds of dollars a week.

A few minutes later everyone was in place. "Man 1," David said into the walkie-talkie."

"Man 1," the former ranger confirmed.

"Man 2," David intoned.

"Man 2," the former green beret confirmed.

"Man 3," David said.

"Man 3," his buddy from JSOC confirmed.

"Man 4," David said into his talkie.

"Man 4," Coley said.

It's good to hear Coley's voice, David thought. It was good to be there with his buddy especially given all the secrecy David had been required to maintain (even against his old, old friend).

"Man 5," David said.

"Man 5," Reggie Stone said into the talkie.

"Man 6," David said.

"Man 6," the only female in Special Ops Aviation said back. David thought it was critical to have a woman there. He couldn't bear to think about it, but he knew there was a chance Tommie could be traumatized from abuse, even sexual abuse. Law enforcement officials had long known that female victims of abuse often react negatively, even wildly, at the sight and sound of more men, even men there to help them, and David had seen it personally. Plus, Special Ops Aviation Lt. Jolie was good. Everybody said so—even the men. Lt. Jolie was one of the few women anyone knew—who had been through SERE, the only Survival, Evasion, Resistance, and Escape training program in the United States where real physical and mental abuse is reputed to occur.

"Miami?" David said.

"Miami," four voices returned.

"Man 7?" David said speeding up now.

"Man 7," Joe Peirinase said into his talkie.

But no one knew that the coordinate Joe entered in the grid from the wrong amount of sale on pump number seven had put Joe on the wrong side of the building.

"On my count, we're hot," David said. He watched the digits of his watch change 5, 4 ,3 ,2 . . . .

"Go, go, go, go!" David commanded into his walkie talkie. Ten men and one woman stormed into the bright small-plane hangar, a tenth of a second apart, some through the roof, some through windows. They hurried to their prearranged positions and waited for their command.

"Man 7, Man 7," David yelled into his talkie as he tore through the hangar, "where the hell are you?"

Only the static of the talkie answered.

"Man 7, Man 7," David hissed into the talkie again, both angry that Joe was not there, and concerned that someone had gotten to him. Four men dressed in army fatigues, helmets, and ski masks sprayed automatic weapons fire in wild directions. One of them spun all the way around, aiming his weapon at something he heard behind him. Joe's unknowable misfire at the gas station landed him almost barrel to barrel with one of the kidnappers.

"I wouldn't," Joe said calmly, walking straight toward the man, weapon raised. "I'm in a really bad mood."

David and the team were able to gauge where Joe was from the nearby gunfire. Joe ran to catch up with the team, ignoring David's voice on the walkie talkie.

"What the fuck happened?"

"Not now!"

David knew that. Adrenaline was pushing through him like never before—not even in the midst of unruly crowds in which the President insisted on mingling (even in foreign countries).

"On the floor, on the floor, on the floor!" the crew commanded and the kidnappers were all face down on the concrete floor with the boots of David's crew in the smalls of their backs and on their heads. The element of surprise had worked; either the kidnappers had no intelligence that they were coming or they were not ready when they arrived.

David pushed his weapon into the back of the first guy's neck. "You have one second to tell me where she is," he seethed, "one-thous...."

"I don't know," the guy yelled back, but before his mouth formed to make the "w" at the end of the word, David blew the back of his head off. Blood poured out of his neck, ears, head, and streamed downward and across the uneven floor causing the man next to him to catch a little blood in his mouth before he had a chance to realize what was happening and turn his face away.

Now standing over the next guy, David said, "You have one second to tell me where she is. Choose your answer wisely."

"Stack!" Coley shouted, "have you lost your fuckin' mind?"

David's crew looked at each other with raised eyebrows. No one was supposed to come out of the bag like that, especially not David. And Coley knew not to use anyone's name; it just came out.

"I-I-I," the man began but before he could get *"I don't know"* out of his mouth David cocked his gun.

"Are you sure you want to ride this train, son?" David seethed.

Coley, Joe, and Reggie exchanged worried glances. They were all covering these men—they had them under control. But if they moved toward David to prevent the second shot, their advantage might be lost. The operational clock was ticking.

David started to count again when the man yelled, "In the back, in the back, in the back!" motioning his head in the direction Joe had come from.

"Show me!" David demanded, yanking the guy up by the back of his shirt and flipping him around in front of him.

"Show me!" David yelled again, pushing the guy in front of him with his gun.

Lt. Jolie followed both men towards the far end of the hangar, up a set of stairs, down a hallway, and into a darkened office. The rest of the crew stayed behind, pulling black sheaths over the heads of the kidnappers, and handcuffing the two remaining men together and around a support beam on the right side of the hangar. One of the Miami boys took up his post as a lookout while the rest of David's crew checked out the remainder of the area for others, yelling "clear" after securing each area.

Up the metal staircase and down the hall, David and Lt. Jolie could see a number of what looked like office doors. Almost all the doors were open with lights on that shot a glare down the hallway.

"Which one?" David demanded, "How far down?"

"Last door on the left."

The hallway was wide enough for David, Lt. Jolie, and the kidnapper to walk three across but David pushed the kidnapper ahead of him with the nose of his gun while holding him at the collar. The hallway curved a little with the building.

"How much further?" David yelled. He was losing patience and time.

"About twenty more feet," the kidnapper replied, out of breath from the awkward way David was marching him down the hallway.

Downstairs, things were under control, but all the men were worried about the time that was passing. And what David had done. *What the fuck?!*

CHAPTER THIRTY-FOUR

David slowed as the kidnapper directed him towards the room where Tommie was allegedly being held. One door before, he had pushed the kidnapper to the floor, zip-tied his wrists over his head to the doorknob and stuffed the red paisley bandana into his mouth.

"If you try to move, or make any noise, I'll shoot you in the head," David growled. He smacked him in the side of his head with his gun butt, for good measure.

But now, in the doorway, Tommie's doorway, David froze. Tommie was lying on the floor, unconscious. Her arms and feet were bound tightly with electrical tape. She was blindfolded, and she had on fatigues, like her captors.

They took her clothes off.

David tried to force out of his head the scenario that surely would have cast loose what little mind Coley thought David had left. David wanted to scoop her up in his arms, like he'd done a hundred times before, and take her away from whatever torment they had put her through, but his professional training told him that he would need to approach her quietly, if quickly, and gauge her mental and physical state first. He knelt beside her and tried to see if anything looked injured or broken. Lt. Jolie knelt beside her on the other side, facing her.

Agent Stackhouse and Lt. Jolie had decided on that together. That they would both approach her gently to give Tommie whatever she might need. The closeness and security of the man she knew so well, or the comfort and easiness of a woman who might better understand what she had gone through.

"Tommie," David said softly.

She didn't answer. After removing her binds, David slid his arms underneath her and started to lift her gently. Tommie moaned but her eyes didn't open. It was not the moan David was used to hearing. Once he was standing with Tommie in his arms, he motioned with his head toward the door to the office.

Lt. Jolie squeezed Tommie's arm gently, and whispered, "Tommie, I'm here."

Tommie's eyelids flittered, then opened towards the familiar voice, toward Lt. Jolie.

"Hi, Jo," Tommie's weak voice barely breathed out.

"You know each other?" David said.

"I was just trying to be comforting by using her name. You know that tactic well, Agent Stackhouse."

"She called you 'Jo,'" David said annoyed that Lt. Jolie would keep something like that from him.

"Agent Stackhouse, she's hallucinating, or something. We do not know each other, I assure you."

David was far from convinced, but he would have to deal with it later. They only had a few minutes before the sticks they placed around the building would blow and the fire alarm would trigger. Lt. Jolie released the man who led them to Tommie from his bindings and pushed him forward with the nose of her weapon. Downstairs, the rest of the team was escorting the other men through a side door of the hangar to their vehicles.

David said into his talkie, "Air 1, we're on the move. Air 2, you're out."

David had arranged for two helicopters but with only four kidnappers total, he cut the second one loose. The man David killed was still lying on the floor in the middle of the hangar. A long trail of blood followed the line of the uneven floor all the way to one side near where Coley had crashed through the windows. Coley met David right in front of the dead man.

"What do you want to do about this?" Coley asked. He was almost afraid of the answer. David leaned down, still holding Tommie in his arms, and pulled the man's ski mask back. He looked for a long time, it seemed to Coley.

Juror number seven.

"Let him burn," David said and walked away with Tommie in his arms.

CHAPTER THIRTY-FIVE

Minutes later, David was in the helicopter with Tommie and a military doctor, fire trucks were screaming toward the hangar, and the crew was dark. While the doctor examined Tommie, David called the President on his private number.

"I got her," David said into the phone, barely waiting for the President to answer.

"And?"

"We're on our way to Bethesda Naval, the doctor's looking at her now," David said.

"But is she all right?" the President persisted.

"Mr. President, she's alive," David said. He knew that the President was asking for more specific details, signs of abuse or torture. But at this moment, to David, that Tommie was alive was all that mattered. "She's unconscious," David finally explained, "but there don't appear to be broken limbs or other outward signs of abuse."

"Update me ASAP, Agent Stackhouse."

"Of course, sir. Thank you, sir," David said trying to convey the depth of his appreciation for the President's support.

"I will update the team here."

The President had purposefully not asked Agent Stackhouse any details about the mission, and David purposefully had not offered any.

"Sheldon," the President answered his private line.

"I thought you would want to know, Mr. President," a female voice said.

"I think Tommie is going to be okay."

"How do you know?" the President asked.

"She recognized me. She called me 'Jo,'" Lt. Jolie said to President Pierce.

"That's our girl," the President said. Lt. Jolie could hear the President's smile in his voice.

"Yes, sir," Lt. Jolie said, and they were both gone.

The President called down to the Situation Room and informed the agents in charge that the mission was over, that Tommie had been found, and that he would brief them in more detail in the coming days.

His relief was all-consuming. There hadn't been enough time, he didn't think, for any of the knowledge Tommie had about his project to be extracted. He could not remember ever feeling so tired. He got into bed, turned off the lights, and plopped down on the pillow.

I need to reschedule that meeting, the President thought as he drifted off to sleep. *The world is waiting for me to act.*

CHAPTER THIRTY-SIX

"Even though I walk through the shadow of the valley of death, I shall fear no evil."
—PSALMS 23:1-6

Agent Stackhouse watched the President's press conference from Tommie's hospital room. At Bethesda Naval Hospital, Tommie was stable. To everyone's relief, especially David's (he had been inconsolable waiting to hear whether Tommie had been abused sexually), there were no signs of physical or sexual abuse. The toxicology report showed that the sodium pentothal had been mixed with another drug. There were still traces of it in Tommie's system. They could not identify it yet but there wasn't enough left in her to be the speculated cause of her persistent state of unconsciousness.

Tommie was not technically in a coma, but she was in an unconscious state. She responded to sound and touch and light, but she could not speak or open her eyes. All her vital signs were strong, especially her heart, but she remained in a faraway place and they had not been able to bring her back in the many days since her rescue. At least not yet. They had run every test.

She should have come out of it by now, whatever it was. It had been weeks from that day in the briefing room when David first heard those terrible words. Like a needle stuck in a groove in an LP, they had been repeating in his head ever since: "Mr. President, my chief of staff Tommie, is missing. When she didn't make it to work this morning, we went to her house. My agents have just confirmed that it appears that she was kidnapped."

But this was a big day for President Pierce. A historic day. For the country, for the world, and David should have been at the White House. He knew that. He could not leave her, though. He had been visiting Tommie every evening since he rescued her. He hoped the repetitiveness, the routine would somehow familiarize himself to her again and bring her out of whatever dark hole had her trapped. It had not worked so far but he kept it up night after night after night.

The President had told David that he could not wait any longer. He was supportive of the commitment David was paying to Tommie, he encouraged it, but the announcement that he had begun to make that day in the White House, in preparation for his announcement to the world, its time had come.

David was content with that. It would come in time to help Sheila, he thought, and he knew that would be enough for the President.

The President looks regal, David thought, but he didn't know if it was because he knew what he was going to say, or whether the precedence of the announcement conferred an air of preeminence upon him. The Oval Office also looked particularly beautiful with artificial light reflecting in all the right angles. *It's probably just the way the White House Press Office set it up tonight.*

The White House had gone to some length to make this occasion momentous in every way. The press office had spent an inordinate amount of time moving things around, setting chairs in just the right position, resetting them, buying new filters for the bright lights. The press secretary and his deputies had also spent days selecting the right number of reporters to gaggle in the Oval Office. This would be the biggest announcement any President would ever make, bar no issue that had ever arisen or could arise, and the President would have to answer some key questions.

The President's key medical experts and scientists, including men and women from NASA, were on stand-by, prepped to handle some of the more technical concerns, but the President was keenly aware of every step, every stumble, and every climb of this journey.

There was no question the President would have been unable to answer in his own right clearly and accurately. But it was still critical that the White House select the reporters most likely to ask the most thoughtful and least negative, headline-grabbing questions. The press office, and the President, were counting on that and it was critical for the orderly delivery of the message. It was more than likely that chaos would follow such news, and not just chaos in Washington, but around the world.

Indeed. President Pierce had been on the phone personally for hours talking with heads of state around the globe about the importance of his announcement and the need for the anticipation of unrest in their countries. He had to trust that they would accept his representations without learning the actual news. He could not take the chance of a single leak. Even the press office did not know the exact message. The President had worked all night on his address to the nation. By himself.

"Fellow Americans, and ladies and gentlemen around the world," the announcer boomed into the mic, "the President of the United States of America."

David could see all the doctors, nurses, and hospital workers on Tommie's floor gathered in front of the TV sets in the family lounges and empty patients' rooms. Some were even sharing the anticipation with patients who had been recuperating well in their rooms. David held Tommie's hand.

"My fellow Americans," the President began, "tonight I make an announcement that will change the world. It will change the lives of every person on the planet, for the good.

"At no time in history has there ever been an opportunity for a single government to do so much good for so many. I am humbled and I am honored to be in this place at this time with the men and women whose extraordinary work and sacrifice made this day possible.

"But first let me say, it was not without dark days and difficult choices. In the end, when everything is known, some of you will question some of those decisions.

"You should understand that every tough choice was a decision of mine and mine alone. So, when you have those questions, you must remember where the buck stops. It stops with me and I will shoulder the burden of that responsibility.

"I believe these difficult decisions were worth the outcome. Including the decision that I made, and vigorously enforced, to maintain complete confidentiality of our efforts. It was necessary for the science and the success of these efforts. My fellow Americans . . . and citizens of the world. The United States of America has discovered . . . the cure for cancer. All cancer."

David could hear the gasps of people all over the hospital upon hearing the news. And then silence, except for the beeps of the patients' heart monitors and blood pressure machines and other critical care equipment. He hadn't thought of it before but suddenly the irony of him being in a hospital while the President announced the government's ability to save millions of people, maybe hundreds right around him, struck him, and he smiled.

"Hey, Tommie," he said playfully. "You're missing out on one of life's great ironies. You know how you like irony, quirks of fate, paradoxes. Wait, is that a word, paradoxes? Geez, there's another one. Of the two of us, you're the one who would know the answer to that. But you can't talk." He laughed awkwardly, uneasily, nervously. "Anyway, here we are, in a hospital with people all around us fighting against, dying of, breast cancer, and lung cancer, and pancreatic cancer, and cervical cancer, and ... well, you get the point ... while your friend and mine tells the world we can end all of it. Don't you think that's ironical, Sweetie? Okay. Time to get up now. You're missing out. You're miss...."

Agent Stackhouse's voice trailed off as he brought himself back to his reality. Tommie could not share this moment with him, here, or anywhere else. She was miles away from him and he did not know why.

CHAPTER THIRTY-SEVEN

Icarus.

After a few more statements, the President called for questions from the few hand-picked reporters in the Oval Office.

"Yes, Mary," the President said, pointing to Mary Still, a well-reputed, long-serving reporter from the *Washington Post* who had always given the White House a pass on difficult issues when they needed it.

"Yes, thank you, Mr. President," Mary began. "First, congratulations! As you indicated, this is life-altering news for every man, woman, and child in the world. My colleagues and I will have a plethora of questions, of course. But I must ask you, Mr. President. Did this great discovery have anything to do with what happened on U Street?"

The Oval Office was deadly, eerily quiet. It seemed that the question had even silenced the clicking of the cameras. Then they began again feverishly.

"Mary, I have to confess, I had hoped you'd ask a different question. When it would be available, perhaps, or are there side effects, or how will it be delivered, questions like that," the President began, finally breaking the fragile quiet. "But you asked the question, and I must be honest.

"No," the President lied.

Cameras clicked wildly as the sea of notepad bearing hands stabbed the air.

"Mr. President, Mr. President. . . ."

"What about Mississippi? Any connection there, Mr. President?"

"No," the President lied.

"The President and his key advisors on this will be conducting a lengthy press conference at eight o'clock, tomorrow. All of your questions will be answered then," the White House press secretary interjected, ending the announcement.

It had gotten off track with those questions, but the President and his staff had contemplated that, and they were prepared.

"In the meantime, please refer to the press packet my deputy is handing you now. Thank you and goodnight."

The press pool was in shock. Everyone was. The White House had counted on that.

CHAPTER THIRTY-EIGHT

"Oh, my God!" Nicki exclaimed to Shep before he had even said hello. "Are you watching this?"

"Of course. Everybody on Earth is watching this."

"That is some wild fucking shit, don't you think? I mean, the government curing cancer? Do you think they really did?"

"Look, you know as well as anyone how I feel about the federal government. I don't trust any of 'em as far as I can throw 'em. But I sure as hell don't think the President of the United States is going on national—no, international TV—telling the world we cured cancer, if we hadn't. Plus, they obviously did some questionable stuff to get there or he would not have set up the whole thing about 'choices' and 'sacrifices.' We were supposed to be years away from a cure—decades. But I absolutely believe the government would think it was okay to do some things most people wouldn't otherwise have it do, if it was going to do something good."

"Whew! That's all I can say. Makes you think how unimportant, and, by comparison trifling, the day-to-day stuff we do is."

"I guess if there was a time to get philosophical about something, it's now," Shep chuckled.

"I wonder if it has anything to do with what they found at U Street?"

"I would say cloning human parts would be something most people wouldn't want our government doing for sure. I hope not for the government's sake. This country is made up of skeptics. If people thought something as ghastly as what happened at U Street related to a cure for cancer, many wouldn't trust it, or take it, or whatever it's going to be."

"No doubt about that."

"You're right though. That's some wild shit."

Nicki laughed but when she got off the phone with Shep, all she could think of was how dreadful it would be if there was a connection. No one ever reasonably explained U Street, no one in authority anyway.

Just then Nicki's cat leaped into her arms.

"Hey, Stoli girl! What do you think? You think the prez's announcement has anything to do with U Street and the cloning? Yes, of course, you're right. It's the only thing that makes sense, I mean, it's been a long time since the government sponsored medical experiments, in the name of important science, on unaware, vulnerable patients, killing thousands of them. But if you had a choice between killing a few people to save millions, wouldn't you do it? It's a dilemma, Stoli girl, isn't it? A moral dilemma of the highest nature. Sure glad I didn't have to decide that shit," Nicki said moving Stoli from her lap and placing her on the bed next to her. "Aren't you glad we didn't have to decide that shit?"

Stoli didn't answer.

CHAPTER THIRTY-NINE

"The ultimate measure of a man is not where he stands in moments of comfort and convenience, but where he stands at times of challenge and controversy."
—DR. MARTIN LUTHER KING, JR.

The White House Situation Room was teeming with activity after the President's announcement. The Task Force President Pierce assembled to deal with the enormity of the announcement had been working secretly for months in preparation for this day. Headed by the President's Surgeon General and the Director of NIH, it was now running full-out.

To prevent leaks, it had been run like a terrorist cell. Where overlap or coordination was not required, members operated in silos, largely unaware of what other members were working on, or even who the other members were. The doctors responsible for discovering and developing the cocktail of medicines that stopped and reversed the activity of cancer cells, and those who would take the drug to market, that chain could not be broken. But that group was happily uninvolved with the group of doctors and scientists whose job it would be to prioritize the delivery of the drug to individual patients.

Indeed, anyone who had indicated an enthusiastic willingness to play God in this way was automatically disqualified from consideration. The President was concerned, rightly, that anyone who would volunteer to make judgments about which dying cancer victims got the cure first, and which waited, had the wrong orientation. That might have been the wrong analysis, but no one involved was comfortable with the idea. So that group, cynically and distastefully dubbed "the widow makers," was hand-picked by the President, one-by-one, after exhaustive vetting, a two-day face-to-face interview with the President himself, and a lot of psychological testing by other doctors selected by the President.

The smallest factors, and the largest, got candidates eliminated from consideration. One doctor, a world-renowned brain surgeon whose success rate was so high some of his peers believed his surgical skills were gifted by God, was rejected because when the White House butler brought coffee and tea into the Oval Office during his meeting, he failed even to acknowledge his service, much less say thanks. What President Pierce saw in this was not just rudeness. It was a total disregard of another human being, a complete inability to connect with another person. The President wanted the men and women charged with making life and death decisions to do it based as much on the value of a life as on the science.

It had been a huge debate. No one involved thought the President should visit upon those doctors the burden of such subjectivity; especially not into a process already so fragile, difficult, and complicated. The Task Force's experts argued that only the most objective factors could be used in determining the priority of drug delivery, both to take the whole playing-God thing out of the process, and to assure the public that the process was impartial and fair.

The President had agreed with the importance of these outcomes, of course, but he argued that any doctor who made a medical decision based solely on the science ignored the mind-body connection to wellness, something he believed in profoundly. How could one explain, he argued, the medical "miracles" that happened every day, the patients who were not supposed to ever walk again, or even live. In the end, the President won the argument. The President always wins the argument, in the end.

It was also the President's direction to run the Task Force like a terrorist cell. He had spent years studying and learning about how they work and had long thought there was an end to which the model could be employed for the greater good. Years ago, he had even personally debriefed a covert agent who had embedded in a cell, not for the purpose of understanding the facts of that investigation—he let the military do their thing on that—but to learn more about their operations. Of course, President Pierce did not talk to his Task Force members about employing a terrorist cell model. He just did it, quietly, in his organized and authorization process. He well knew the stakes involved in disclosure of his plan. Under any other name, the model might have been evaluated, even criticized, fairly and objectively—on the merits of its operation. Any association to the words "terrorist cell," he knew, would preclude any rational consideration of the idea, or meaningful support of the project. So, no one knew about it, though members of his cabinet alluded to it unwittingly that day in the Roosevelt Room. No one knew about it except Agent Stackhouse. He was the one who had suggested it to the President.

All of this was what the President meant when he said the buck stopped with him. However, as it went, there was no "plausible deniability."

CHAPTER FORTY

As planned, President Pierce went straight to the residence after the announcement. Get him out of the fray, was the thinking. Let the crazies come out with their conspiracies at the front of the story; that way, when the verifiable details came out, it would help make the crazies look even crazier. Besides, there were plenty of advisors who could deal with the big issues until the morning press conference. And that was fine with President Pierce. He had never gotten ahead of the sleep demons, not with all the things that had been happening. He was tired. He laid on the bed and closed his eyes.

I'll just rest a little, he thought. He had just dozed off when his handheld buzzed across the nightstand. It was a pin-to-pin, encrypted text from Sheila: How soon will it be available?

I'll call her tomorrow, the President thought. *Her Washington-insider self is just dying to know the details before anyone else,* he laughed out loud before getting up and getting ready for bed. He had no idea how unaware he was of what Sheila's text portended and anyway, eventually he would have to tell her that he had authorized the cloning of Abby's DNA in the quest for the cure.

CHAPTER FORTY-ONE

"Agent Stackhouse? Sir?"

Tommie's doctor was making his rounds and found David asleep in the chair beside her bed. The nurses found him like that a lot.

"Yes, yes!? Oh, Doctor Grippi, nice to see you."

"You need to get some rest, Agent."

"How does she look, how are things going?"

"Well, we didn't learn much more from the last round of tests. Everything that should be working is working the way it's supposed to be. By all of Tommie's vitals, by all accounts, she should be awake. She should not be in this half-way-in, half-way-out state. I have to ask this, and I hate to, but is there anything that we've missed?"

It was the doctor's way of gently asking David if he knew something about her or her condition that he had not shared with the doctors.

"No, no, nothing that I can think of. I've been racking my brain about it, doctor. You know, she's always had fitful dreams, but she never talks about them."

David gave up the pretense of a "friend" relationship with Tommie shortly after the doctors were unable to wake her up. He knew everything in a case like this was important. He didn't care about the consequences anyway. Obviously.

"Tell me more about the dreams," Dr. Grippi asked, sitting down. "When does she have them? Have you noticed a pattern? Does she say anything? Does she move around?"

"You know, I've been looking for a pattern for a year or so now, something related to food, or work stress, or ... but I just haven't seen anything. There seems to be no trigger, but I know from our training that there's always a trigger."

David had long felt frustrated that he couldn't help Tommie more with her demons. "Anyway, yes, she sometimes speaks but it's unintelligible largely, and often she flails wildly."

"Describe the flailing? Does she use both arms? Are her arms outstretched, punching?"

"All of it. Sometimes she looks like she's just talking with her hands, but sometimes she looks like she's fighting someone off. Like she's had combat training, but of course she hasn't."

"Hm. And you've never been able to make out any words?"

"No, nothing other than saying 'no!'"

"Could she be using a different language, a dialect?"

"Well, she speaks a little French, but not that well anymore . . . no, it just sounds like gibberish."

"Well, that's something," Dr. Grippi said. "I'd been thinking that it's time to bring in a psychiatric specialist to try some exercises."

David had been regretting that eventuality, but he understood too that it was time.

"Of course."

"I'll schedule a visit for tomorrow. If we don't see something from that, I think we will need to inform Tommie's family what's going on, David. I know you have hoped to get her through this without worrying them, but I feel uncomfortable proceeding without the input of immediate family involvement. At this point. Also, I think that can help."

"Yes, yes, of course."

David knew too that he could not put off informing Tommie's family about what was going on any longer. As it was, it would have been unusual, he imagined, for her not to be in touch with them for any length of time.

"Thank you, Doctor. I personally appreciate your time and effort with Tommie."

"Of course, Agent Stackhouse. But do get some rest. You know we will call you the moment there is any change. All the nurses know to do so."

"Thank you. I'll just sit for a little while longer."

"You know you've made a couple of the nurses envious of your dedication to Tommie," Dr. Grippi said warmly as he moved toward the door. "And I think a couple of their husbands are holding you responsible." He had hoped to give David something to smile about, even for a moment.

"Yes, some of the ladies have mentioned it," David laughed. "Thanks again, Doc. Have a good evening. Oh hey, Doc," David called out while the door was swinging closed.

"Yes?" Dr. Grippi caught the door just in time to peek his head through.

"What did you think about the President's announcement this evening?"

"I think it's about time."

CHAPTER FORTY-TWO

"You will know the truth..."
—JOHN 8:32

President Pierce woke up before sunrise the next morning. The day before had been eventful to be sure, but this day, he and his top advisors were going to explain to the world how scientists finally arrested the most insidious of killer diseases, how their discoveries had probable application in any number of other areas including spinal cord detachment, and at least some catastrophic brain injuries. It would be his legacy, the country's legacy, and he had convinced himself that "without darkness, nothing comes to birth."

That government scientists had been able to use human genome sequencing to connect the dots in cell retardation and regeneration came as a surprise to everyone. Completed in 2003, the Human Genome Project, or HGP, coordinated by the Department of Energy and NIH, spent years identifying all the approximately twenty to fifty thousand genes in human DNA, sequencing the three billion chemical base pairs that make up human DNA, and storing the information in secure databases for scientific analysis. Several countries had made major contributions to the project, including the U.K., Japan, France, Germany and, importantly, China. There had been a relatively smooth transfer of related technologies to the private sector and a robust look at the ethical, legal, and social issues involved in such work.

It was a big deal, but experts predicted that analyses of the data that could lead to major medical breakthroughs would take many more years, maybe decades. And it might have. But when President Pierce learned that the Chinese had already cloned human body parts, and that such cloning could be used to conduct the necessary trials and studies to test a real cure for cancer in humans, he felt he had to act.

The ELSI, the HGP's study of those ethical, legal, and social issues surrounding the availability of genetic information related to gender, race, patient care, and the like, demonstrated the variety of expert opinions on the issues. The debate on cloning had been even hotter. Once he decided to take this path, President Pierce was acutely aware that *his* project would have to be conducted secretly.

As he dressed, he practiced his remarks, and mooted himself with tough questions. He called for breakfast in the Yellow Oval, a large room in the residence that captured the true beauty, and historical significance, of the White House. Momentous decisions had been made in that room over the decades, President Pierce knew, many that the American people ultimately learned about—and many they did not.

"Mr. President?" one of his residence agents asked as he entered the room. "I hate to disturb you, sir, but Ms. Sheila Cooper is at the Northwest Gate. She says she must see you."

The agent was uncomfortable reporting to the President that an unscheduled visitor, especially this morning, was insisting on seeing him, but instincts told the uniform division agents at the gate that she should not be turned away.

"It's no problem at all, agent, have her escorted up here."

"Up here, sir?"

"Yes, agent, up here. And have the residence staff come by and see if she wants to join me for breakfast."

Suddenly, President Pierce remembered Shelia's text message and understood that it was more than curiosity.

"Yes, sir, Mr. President."

It took a few minutes for Sheila to get to the Yellow Oval, and by the time she arrived the President had finished eating and was drinking his coffee by the picturesque windows overlooking the White House grounds.

"Mr. President," Sheila said entering the room. "Sam."

"It's good to see you, Sheila. So good to see you. Can I get you anything? Have a seat."

They sat in the two overstuffed chairs in the nook by the window. They could see the sun almost halfway up now in the sky, and it cast a beautiful shadow on the Washington Monument. President Pierce noticed how gingerly Sheila had eased into her chair.

"Sam, I don't want to seem ill-mannered or discourteous, I know how big a day this is for you, for the country. And I certainly don't want to put you in an awkward position; I've done that enough for a lifetime, I suspect."

Sheila had never gotten over her guilt about Abby. Certainly, when she considered keeping Abby, she hadn't anticipated that then-Sheldon would become President Pierce, and she had every intention of raising Abby alone. Things just hadn't worked out that way.

"But I need to ask..."

"Sheila, what is it? Are you sick?"

Sheila hadn't intended to tell President Pierce about her illness until she had no other choice, and she didn't expect that to be for some months. But now, with the possibility she might live through it, she knew the sooner she got help. the better for everyone. Especially Abby.

"I have pancreatic cancer, Sam. There is no cure, well... there was no cure. I..."

President Pierce was already leaning toward a gentle hug around Sheila. "We can fix it, Sheila. We can make you better. We can cure you."

"I was hoping you'd say that."

Sheila was relieved but she was surprised by the fatigue left by her reprieve. "Abby doesn't know. I have just recently started to show symptoms. I think. But it won't be long before she—"

"Sheila, I need to tell you something too. This has been..."

Just then the secure phone rang.

"Yes?" the President answered.

"Mr. President, are you ready? We'd like to go over a few things that happened in the news overnight, before the press conference."

"I'll be down shortly," the President said to his chief of staff.

"Go ahead, Sam. Here are the names and numbers of my doctors at Johns Hopkins," Sheila said handing the President a handwritten piece of paper. "Just have someone on your staff let them know what I should do, if there is somewhere I should go, you know—whatever the protocol is. I'll be fine. Now."

"We have a few minutes, Sheila. I do want to tell you about—"

"Sam, you need to go. And, I need to go. I don't need to be seen here once everything gets crazy. Whatever it is, I'm sure it can wait."

The President was uncomfortable not sharing his secret with Sheila, especially now. But now that he knew about Sheila, he wasn't sure if it would have been the right thing to tell her today. Maybe ever.

The White House Briefing Room, much smaller in person, was as tightly packed as it had ever been. The press secretary, an unusual veteran of both Democratic and Republican White Houses, had supervised the delivery of three-inch binder press packets to everyone in the room. One idea was to bury the press with paper, an irony not lost on anyone in the press office. Another was to provide every answer to every possible question, in writing, just a few minutes in advance of the conference so that many questions could be answered by referring them to their packets.

"Ladies and gentlemen, the President of the United States..."

CHAPTER FORTY-THREE

"There is no greater agony than bearing the untold story inside you."
—ZORA NEALE HURSTON, DUST TRACKS ON A ROAD

"Tommie. I'm Doctor Graves. I'm here to help you get back from wherever you are."

Dr. Grippi had arranged for the psychiatric team to see Tommie first thing in the morning. He had learned from the nurses that Agent Stackhouse was settling in for another night and he figured early morning would be a good time to begin the session; David usually left just before dawn to shower and change.

Tommie was connected to all kinds of probes and clicking machines. It was just as well that David did not see her that way. Dr. Graves, an internationally known brain doctor at Bethesda Naval, was convinced that something had traumatized Tommie into a semi-conscious state; a place where she could be where no one could hurt her.

"Thomasina, Thomasina," she soothed as she reviewed the printouts of her brain activity. The probes were doing more than just monitoring brain waves. Tiny probes strategically placed pulsed rhythmic vibrations in designed sequences on her wrists, the bottom of her feet, and behind her ears. Dr. Graves had conducted this protocol hundreds of times. It was a combination of modern-day electric shock and acupuncture—East meets West—and it usually worked. Quickly.

"No, no . . . we have to complete the mission. We have to complete the mission. I'm fine."

"Tommie, who are you talking to?" Dr. Graves asked.

"LT."

"Who is LT?"

"My husband. Detective Lawrence Tyler."

Dr. Graves knew Tommie wasn't married but she saw this frequently. Physiologically impaired patients often mixed up or fantasized people, relationships, etc. It was a common side-effect of trauma.

"How long have you and Mr. Tyler been married," Dr. Graves continued. It was important to continue down the path the patient began because that was where they would be found, at least in their minds.

"Shhhhh . . . ." Tommie said putting an involuntary forefinger over her mouth. "We're not really married, we're undercover married," she giggled.

The procedure had relaxed Tommie's mind and imposed a drunk-like state.

"Ah!" Doctor Graves said offering her support. It was important for patients in this state to feel believed and supported. "What's your real name, then?"

"Thomasina L. Coles."

The fact that Tommie offered her real name was significant. It signaled that her statements were truthful, albeit confused, the doctor knew.

"What do you do, Ms. Coles? Who do you work for?" Dr. Graves was less interested in probing Tommie's personal life than helping her defeat her demons. It was the only way she would wake up.

"The CIA!" Tommie barked. Then quickly slurred, "Shhhhhhhhhh."

"Tommie, Tommie what are you talking about?" David asked, incredulous. He had just gone for coffee, and he had opened the door in time to hear Tommie say "CIA."

"Agent, please, this is a very delicate situation," Dr. Graves said. "It is not appropriate for you to be in here."

David had been eavesdropping outside of Tommie's door. He had arrived shortly after the doctor began. No one had to tell him what he was doing was inappropriate. He knew that acutely.

"Tommie, it's David!" he demanded.

"Agent, I must ask you to leave."

Tommie's blood pressure monitor was going through the roof.

"Tommie, are you really CIA? Is that how you knew Lt. Jolie back in the warehouse?"

Suddenly, things made sense. The kidnapping, President Pierce's urgency in getting her back, that moment between Tommie and Lt. Jolie.

Tommie's eyes were still closed but her finger found her lips again, "Shhhhhhh."

David shook his head, turned on his heels, and left Tommie, her doctor, her demons, her past . . . all of it, behind.

CHAPTER FORTY-FOUR

"What's up man?" Coley said walking toward David at one of their regular spots. David was already there waiting for him.

"Wow man, you look like shit. How's Tommie? She any better?"

There was a long silence. Coley decided it was better not to fill it with small talk; he just let Agent Stackhouse take his time. And then he saw something he had never seen before. Tears.

"Tommie's CIA. She's been covert for I don't know how long. She's even played the wife. You know what that shit means," David said, choking up.

"Wait a minute. Let's not jump the gun here. I assume you know the CIA thing is a fact. But anything else is pure speculation."

David did not speak again for a long time. When he did, he was already starting to get up from the bench. He didn't really know if the CIA thing was accurate but everything in his mind now screamed that it was. It was the only answer to a million questions.

"That's what I'm afraid of, Jim. That our whole relationship is just speculation. Or worse; just a job."

"Okay, okay, let's go have a drink," Coley said. "You're talking crazy. That girl adores you and you know it."

Coley had never seen his friend like that; he did not intend to leave him.

"A drink? Man, it's 10:30 in the morning."

"Coffee then?" Coley tried.

"I don't want coffee, Jim," David said, rising now from the bench they were sitting on. Agent Stackhouse nodded to Coley and headed toward

246

the Jefferson Memorial. Coley watched as David walked with his head down and his hands in his pockets.

Should I go after him? Do we need to talk about the op?

Coley decided it was better to give his friend some space, for now, but he did not for one moment intend to leave him alone about this. There were too many unanswered questions, too much emotion, too much at stake. It wasn't until Coley got up to leave himself that he noticed it. David had left his sidearm, his badge, and his White House credentials right there on the bench.

CHAPTER FORTY-FIVE

"... And the truth will set you free."
—JOHN 8:32

Nicki was watching the President's second-day press conference as she got dressed for work. She had an easy day—no court appearances, and her next trial wasn't for sixty days. She pulled on her jeans, a white t-shirt, her black leather jacket. The President and his advisors were averting a lot of the questions with the referral to the press packet and some of the journalists were getting frustrated. This was the story of a lifetime; the President said he and his advisors would take questions, and instead he was deflecting them left and right.

"That's what I would do," she said to Stoli. "If I could say I cured cancer, or found life on the moon, or any of the biggies, I wouldn't tell people jack if I didn't want to," she laughed.

As she headed downstairs, Stoli in tow, and switched on the TV in the kitchen, Nicki's cell phone skidded across the counter.

A text message from an unknown number: I'm at your front door.

Should I text back, she thought. *Would texting back even work?*

Just then, the doorbell rang.

"Nik, it's me," Detective Tyler said into the door.

They hadn't talked since just after the trial and Nicki was comfortable with that. She didn't know what was going on in his life, he didn't seem to want to tell her, and she was too old to play James Bond spy games with him, she'd told Stoli one tear-filled night after the trial.

"What's goin' on, now?" Nicki asked opening the door.

"I feel like I owe you some answers, Nicki, and I can finally give them to you."

"It's too late, Lawrence. I don't care anymore. The trial is over, the President has a cure for cancer, all is right in my world."

But that wasn't the truth. Nicki had been badgering Shep for weeks to find out what Det. Tyler was doing in that alley with Mrs. Campbell, what that horror show was on U Street, and whether the courtroom shooter really was some nut who just happened to pick the most eventful trial going on in the courthouse that day.

Shep had figured out some of it. He knew that Det. Tyler was more than a police detective and that he'd spent a number of years overseas. One of Shep's buddies from the Gulf War had met him on a mission. Shep had also gotten that young officer who was charged with getting the courtroom officials out of danger and downtown that day to sneak him the preliminary police report on the shooting. It wasn't the case of a nutcase at all. It was related to Tyler, not in his capacity as a detective, but as a covert agent. But they had only been able to spin big tales about U Street, and Nicki had no expectation of getting that out of Lawrence.

"I don't believe you don't care, Nik. I know it's been a long time, but I know you better than that. Plus, I know your investigator has been snooping around at your behest."

"Fine, then. Solve the puzzle. Answer all the questions. Connect all the dots."

"Can we sit down and talk to each other like human beings?"

Nicki still had mixed emotions about Lawrence. She had loved him once, deeply. But now, his word was compromised, and she did not trust him.

"Fine," she sniped. "Coffee?"

"Thanks." Det. Tyler appreciated Nicki's conciliation.

Nicki disappeared into the kitchen, and Lawrence decided to follow her. She turned towards him with a steaming cup. She thrust it into his hands and looked at him expectantly.

"U Street was a rogue scientist who had been assigned to the President's Task Force on this cancer stuff. As far as we can tell, he decided he wanted to make the discovery himself, and he stole specimens, protocols, a little bit of everything, it looks like, and started his own 'lab.'"

We?

"I guess he'd seen too many movies. He picked a row house on U Street because of some hiding-in-plain sight theory. Anyway, we think the isolation, and the lawlessness, fried his brain and he started doing crazy experiments that resulted in the Stephen King horror you heard about. It was a mess. Just a mess. And poor Mrs. Campbell was one of the macabre results. This guy, this now mad scientist . . . "

"That's not funny."

"You're right. Sorry. Anyway, this guy got in his head that he needed some more human organs to work on and he hired those thugs to get them however they could. But the thugs he hired were stupid, and vicious, and poor Mrs. Campbell suffered the horrendous consequences of his madness, and their inhumanity. But that's why I was there. We had a tip, and I was following it."

"*We?* We think the isolation . . . *we* got a tip? How do you know all of this, Lawrence?"

"Look, Nik, I know Shep told you that I've been an operative and all of that. Well, the President brought me back from overseas to help him with the Task Force. On the security/protection side."

There was a long pause before Nicki spoke. Detective Tyler gave her the time. As she pretend-busied herself getting more coffee, LT discreetly looked around the kitchen for old memories.

"So, you know all about what the President is talking about today?"

"Not all. I don't think anybody knows all of it but the President. But a lot of it, yes."

"And the courtroom shooting?"

Det. Tyler could hear the incredulity in Nicki's voice. It was quite a story, he knew, but Nicki was connecting the dots in her head. The truth was it was the only story that made any sense.

"That was about me. It was a warning. People weren't supposed to be killed, apparently. It was a warning to me that my silence was still required. On another matter."

Nicki turned her head towards the TV. The press conference, in its second hour now, was winding up. The President looked tired but pleased.

"Well, what do you think?" she said after a long quiet.

"About what?"

"About everything."

"I don't know, Nik. If you could save tens of millions of lives, maybe give people their legs back, how far would you go?"

"That's the question isn't it? "

"Actually," Nicki said, "the question is ... how far did the President go?"

CHAPTER FORTY-SIX

Nicki was trying to reach Shep when her call-waiting clicked in. "Hello?"

"Hey Nicki, it's Reggie. What's up kiddo, how ya' doin?"

"Hi, Reggie. All right, I guess. Head's still spinning a little."

"Yeah. A lot has happened over the last few months. I'm calling to get you out for a drink with old friends. You up for it?"

"What friends?"

"Your friends, my friends. Come on, it'll be fun."

"Where?"

"Our old haunt on fifteenth."

"Stan's? That ol' dive?"

"It's an oldie but a goodie. "

Nicki laughed. "What time?"

"Whenever you get here."

"You're already there? I don't hear any noise."

"I'm out front but everyone else is inside. See you shortly."

Stan's *was* a dive, inside and out. Barely visible from the street, the entrance and egress were the same—a narrow nearly vertical set of concrete stairs that descended a quarter story below the sidewalk. It was small, dark and before the smoking ban, a place where cigarette and cigar plumes competed with the smell of strong drinks and sweaty men. Now only the men—and some of the women—smelled like cigs and cigars, but they were still as boisterous and profane. It was known largely to law enforcement and military types; too many secrets had been spilled over too many drinks there. One, decades before, had brought down a president.

Reggie watched out for Nicki's arrival and when she pushed on the door handle, he was already on the other side of it. He wanted to ease her into the get-together but out of the corner of her eye, in the back, in the dark, she had already made out Shep. And Agent Stackhouse.

"Whoa! What have you gotten me into?"

"Like I said, drinks with friends."

"Ms. Lewis," David said extending his hand. "Nice to see you again. Congratulations on the trial."

"Agent Stackhouse," she nodded. "Are we destined always to meet in the dark of night?"

Everyone laughed—even David—and Shep gave Nicki a wink as she eased into her seat.

"Old friends, huh?" she said to Reggie. But she was glad for the company—their company. Reggie ordered a third round for the table, Nicki a Heineken. She looked around to get her bearings and noticed there was only one other woman in the bar.

What a place for a date, she thought.

"To trial wins," Shep said raising his glass toward Nicki.

"To trial wins," Reggie said.

"Thanks. So. How drunk do we have to get before one of you tells me what's up? And how the *fuck* do you guys all know each other?"

"That's my girl," Shep said. "The Diplomat."

"No, that's fair," Agent Stackhouse laughed. "We haven't made Ms. Lewis' life easy over the last several months. Well, you know our world is pretty small. Reggie and I have met over the years in various capacities, and you know Reggie and Shep were both in the Gulf. President Pierce embarked on this journey several years ago, shortly after he took office. He had a passion and commitment about it none of us understood until much later. All of it was classified and there were a limited number of people involved. Only two of us knew everything, me and President

Pierce. I reached out to three people I trusted to help me do my job to support the mission.

"As you now know, the mission was to cure cancer. It was that simple, that ambitious. No one thought it could be done in the timeframe the President wanted but, well, he's the President. I involved Reggie, Detective Tyler, and later Shep in discreet projects related to the larger mission. I met and reached out to Shep only just recently. He's someone we knew had your back, a reputation for discretion, and the judgment we needed. That was particularly important during the trial."

Nicki swung around to Shep, daggers in her eyes. "You knew about this all along?"

"Not all along, Nicki," Shep said soothingly.

"When it counted," Agent Stackhouse said. David did not want Nicki to get bogged down in who knew what when and how it affected her trusted relationships.

"Shep was not permitted to tell you anything, and the less you knew, the safer we believed we could keep you. Trust me, that is the *only* reason he didn't tell you. He was granted a special temporary clearance and after today it will be revoked. Anyway, because Detective Tyler ended up being the main eyewitness in your case, and the role he was playing for us, well . . . it complicated things and situated you smack in the middle of something that didn't have anything to do with you. All we could do at that point was try to protect you and to stay out of the way of the trial. It wasn't always easy."

"And what about that officer in the courtroom that LT fingered?"

"Oh, that was just smoke."

"And U Street?"

"U Street was a real fire. An unfortunate consequence, perhaps of the stress of the mission, or perhaps a missed psychological aberrancy, we're not sure yet. But it was basically the madness of one scientist, one of the specialists we relied on during the medical trials. He caused quite a stir, obviously, and accelerated the President's timetable. But it was just as well, I thought, anyway. It was just a matter of time before we started having leaks."

Agent Stackhouse paused and took a sip of his drink. The noise level at Stan's had risen precipitously as the evening wore on but there, at their little table in the back, in the dark, you could hear a pin drop.

Finally, Nicki spoke again, "So basically, the President of the United States cloned people to hurry up a cure for cancer and it worked."

"I didn't say that, Ms. Lewis. You did."

"Fine, fine, I said it. How long do you think it will be before that gets out?"

"Nicki," Shep said.

"You're right, you're right. Let's get another round and talk about someone else."

"Good idea. How 'bout those Knicks?" Reggie laughed.

Agent Stackhouse had only spoken briefly, and only for those few moments, but for Nicki time seemed to have stopped. Now, again, Nicki could hear the clicking ice cubes and clanging plates and someone let the air back in the room. The four of them joked and laughed about ordinary things until last call. After giving Nicki a hug, Reggie caught up with Agent Stackhouse who had paid the check and was heading down 15th Street toward the White House.

"You have to go back in now?"

"No. I turned in my badge and weapon last week."

"What? Why?"

"Tommie."

"What do you mean? That was a 'clean op,'" he said in air quotes, "and anyway. I hear she's recovering nicely."

"Yeah well, things aren't always what they seem," David said.

He did not say any more, and Reggie didn't press him. Reggie was sure President Pierce would be able to press him back into service after a short break.

David knew better. He was not going back to the White House, or to Tommie. He went to his car, got in it, and headed for the lake. Pieces of a man.

Shep draped an arm around Nicki as they walked up 15th Street. "Why did the President take such a risk to do this?" she asked Shep.

"It's a sad story, actually. You remember that the President was married before, right? She was the love of his life, they say. Anyway, when they were trying to get pregnant, they found out she had ovarian cancer."

"Oh, my."

"When she was on her death bed, she asked him to help find a cure for the terrible cancers that killed women and children, like ovarian and leukemia. She was delirious from the pain meds of course, but he made the promise anyway and when he ended up running for president, well that gave him the first real chance he had of doing it, or at least trying to do it.

"He set up the notion of curing cancer in his very first State of the Union speech, but no one paid it any attention. I mean, it has been such a pipedream, really. Anyway, when Abby came along . . ."

"This is incredible."

"Yeah, well, that's not all. The President learned that cures for different cancers had been close for years but that money, and some risk-taking, stood in the way of real progress. So, he used his presidential powers to get secret funding and set up a huge lab. One day during a briefing one of the scientists let slip that trials would result in faster outcomes if live human tissue could be used. President Pierce got the idea of allowing his secret daughter's DNA to be used for cloning. Just body parts at first. It worked, and they'd already begun manufacturing the drugs that showed success on a small scale in a carved-out space in that plant in Mississippi when . . . ."

"Well, that explains it."

"Yes, that explains the explosion down there. The government was tying up loose ends."

"How does he expect to get away with all of this? I mean some of the things he's done, I don't know, will people give him a pass for it because of the outcome? Will they say the end justified the means?"

"I don't know. It is a big deal. Tens of millions of lives will be saved around the world, not just in America—maybe hundreds of millions. In the end, though, I don't think he cares about the consequences. He fulfilled the promise he made to his dying wife, and he's cured cancer. That's big."

Nicki and Shep had reached his car long before they had gotten to the part about Mississippi, and they were now parked in front of Nicki's house. She was quiet.

"You good?"

"Yeah. I guess. I was thinking about that Langston Hughes short story—you know, the one that goes: '... shoes got by devilish ways will burn your feet.'"

"Yes, ma'am."

———◆———

ACKNOWLEDGEMENTS

So, here's the thing. This novel has been bounding around in my head and—in between careers—my actual life, for a long time. There are many people to thank. Family members, those here and those away, longtime and special friends, mentors, advocates, colleagues. It is my earnest hope, in naming some but not all of you, that I do not cause affront. Certainly, and unquestionably, all of you have my profound gratitude.

Anyway, here it goes...

Thank you Sina, my grandmother, who called me her namesake, and was the definition of love.

Thank you Uncle Adolphus Lewis Jr., an original Tuskegee Airman, who believed I could fly.

Thank you, my other aunts, uncles, cousins, grandparents, and all the play "moms" and "aunts" our extended village comprised.

Thank you, Michele A. Roberts, my friend, and inspiration. I have been in awe of you since we were baby PDs. There would be no Nicki without you.

Thank you, Kim Taylor-Thompson, former Director of the D.C. Public Defender Service, my friend, and inspiration too.

Thank you Randy Stone, my officemate, and the rest of the PDS Class of '83, and all the past and present members of this very special club—the D.C. Public Defender Service.

Thank you, Tree. You have everything to do with the lawyer I became, the lawyer many of us at PDS became.

Thank you, other longtime and special friends, several of whom read early drafts and provided wisdom and constructive but loving criticism: Pammie, Gloria, Ken, Raymond.

Thank you Erik Tarloff for your firm but gentle advice, and your generous help and support.

Thank you, former Congressman Alan Wheat, for your early and continued support, and constructive feedback.

Thank you, Will McCormack, publisher, and Masie Cochran, editor, at Tin House, for your read a couple of years ago, and your wonderful encouragement for me to see this through.

Thank you, Jonathan Groner, for your early copyedit and constructive criticism.

Thank you, George Stephanopoulos, for your long friendship, support, and special encouragement upon reading my manuscript. Your sentiments last year helped me keep going.

Thank you, Judy and Michael Winston, for your friendship, support, and push to get me out of my head and on with it.

Thank you, Greg Jackson for your read, lovely support, and investment in the relationship of two of my favorite characters.

Thank you, Teddy and Ann Burgh at Sweet Read Publishing for believing in me. Thank you Sarah Bode, whose editorial and marketing support have been unsurpassed.

And Sami, my niece and godchild, thank you for your flawless execution of my vision for the powerful cover of my debut novel.

ABOUT THE AUTHOR

LESLIE T. THORNTON has been a Washington, D.C.-based attorney for over 30 years. After growing up in Philadelphia with a twin sister and two older brothers, she began her legal career as a D.C. Public Defender. There, she tried armed rape, murder, and conspiracy cases. Later, Thornton spent eight years as a senior executive in the Clinton Administration. Among other things, Thornton was her agency's representative for the Continuity of Operations of Government plan. Holding a top-secret clearance, Thornton received top-secret national security briefings at "undisclosed locations," and that is all she can say about that! Thornton also worked closely with President Clinton on education and political matters and was Deputy Advisor for the 1996 Presidential Debates. Thornton has received numerous legal awards over her career, but she is perhaps proudest of her recognition from the U.S. Secret Service for her work in creating a permanent partnership between the USSS and the U.S. Department of Education on threat assessment for U.S. schools.

Thornton has been a law partner in two top D.C. law firms, and general counsel for a multi-billion-dollar energy company in charge of nation state actor cyber security for critical infrastructure in Washington, D.C., among other responsibilities. The seriousness of this responsibility led her to return to Georgetown Law for her LL.M in National Security Law. In addition to her legal career, Thornton has served as the only Black woman on the corporate boards of two multi-billion-dollar public companies. Over the years, her opinion pieces have appeared in such publications as *The Wall Street Journal, National Journal/Legal Times, The*

American Lawyer, The Boston Globe, The Washington Times, and *The Daily Oklahoman,* among others.

When she was just 15 years old, Thornton's uncle—an original Tuskegee Airman—taught her how to fly. Or tried to. She had a little trouble with her s-turns.

In the early 2000s, Thornton threw a letter-high strike as the opening pitch at a Nationals game—from the mound. Two years ago, she participated in an operation with the U.S. Secret Service. And that's all she can say about that!

**The adventure continues in the sequel
. . . And the Truth Will Set You Free: A Thriller
by Leslie T. Thornton.
Enjoy this excerpt!**

CHAPTER ONE

"How long has she been awake?"

"Two days. She appears to have full cognitive ability and range. No impairment at all. She's asking for all of *The Washington Post*s since the day she arrived and has been furiously soaking up all the news she can on what the White House has been doing."

"Curiosity?"

"Certainly, we've *all* been glued to the news since the President announced he'd cured cancer, well, not him . . . you know what I mean."

"The nurses say the patient's interest goes well beyond curiosity. Tommie seems to have a special interest. And knowledge."

"What do you mean?"

"I'm not sure what I mean. She's been very quiet. Extremely friendly and cooperative. But very *un*forthcoming."

Doctor Graves laughed. "It's been quite a time, of course, and we have our own challenges and opportunities here at Bethesda Naval. But let's not try to boil the ocean today. Today, let's just see if our patient, the inscrutable Thomasina Coles, is well enough to go home. She's been here long enough."

It was going on the third week since Agent Stackhouse had raced Tommie to the emergency room and Dr. Graves's sessions with Tommie had been intense. Under hypnosis, Tommie had recognition and cognition as well. A picture had begun to emerge of a complex professional and personal life full of holes, ones either she put there, or her condition visited upon her. Dr. Graves had insisted that he be informed the moment she was fully awake, alert and lucid, but the nurse-on-duty failed to read the chart carefully enough to see his instruction and there had been so much activity around her, so many tests after she woke up, no one else noticed either. It wasn't until the morning shift change that the notation was noticed, and Dr. Graves called. Somebody would be getting disciplined over that.

"Good morning, Tommie. I'm Doctor—"

"Graves, yes, I know. How are you?"

"Very happy to see you awake." Doctor Graves took note of how easily Tommie was relating to him, especially given some of the details she'd revealed in therapy, though much of that was under hypnosis. She seemed attentive, but Dr. Graves also noted that Tommie was keeping one of her eyes on cable news. The CNN correspondents were bickering about something big.

"Tommie, can you tell me what you remember about our sessions?"

"Do you mean content-wise, or that we had them?"

Dr. Graves didn't need to hear much more from Tommie to feel comfortable with her condition. Whatever it was that had taken her away from real life, from the reality of her past and present, brought her back with aplomb, self-possession, and ease.

"Whatever you want to share."

"Well, I think I remember a good deal of it. I remember the first day we met, and giggling non-sensibly about being married, or something crazy and, I might add, untrue. I remember—"

"You can't be here!" Dr. Graves interrupted, his pitch high and loud at the same time. A man had just entered the room. "Who are you? How did you get in here, anyway?"

"Ms. Coles, please get dressed, get your things," the man said.

Both Tommie and the doctor could see through the slit of a door window that the man, now walking around, grabbing what looked like personal items and stuffing them in a duffle, was not alone. Another man, with a similarly dark countenance, though shorter and stockier, was standing just outside the door scanning the hallway.

"Doctor, I'm sorry to interrupt," the man said. It was evident he wasn't. "But the President has asked that Ms. Coles be situated under the care of White House physicians immediately. Someone should have informed you; I apologize. Ms. Coles, the President sends his regards."

Dr. Graves didn't buy it. "This is preposterous," the doctor said, "I'm in the middle of a session, Ms. Coles is still very much in a delicate state and no—no one has told me anything. I'd like to see some identification please, and I'll need to inform the chief of the division."

The man in the dark suit, white shirt, clean shaven face, flashed a badge he had no intention of Dr. Graves actually seeing, and indeed, the doctor didn't.

"I didn't catch that, sir. I'm going to need to—"

"It's OK," Tommie said, easing out of the chair and walking, slowly, to the bathroom. For a couple of days now, Tommie had wondered how the CIA was going to get her out for her debrief, and whatever else. *I guess they decided to just gorilla it*, she thought, smiling to herself.

"I don't agree, Tommie. This violates every protocol, and I have no intention of turning you over to strangers who have forced their way into a secure area."

Agent Smith, his badge said, decided it was time to defuse the situation—an escalation would take even more time and attention, neither of which he had the patience for. He stopped collecting items, set the duffle bag on the chair that Tommie had arisen from, sat on the chair's arm, and addressed Dr. Graves.

"Dr. Graves, again, I know this must look and feel, well, wrong. I assure you, the only concern we have is for Ms. Coles's welfare, and we're just following President Pierce's direction. I can try to raise him, if you like, or you can try to reach him through the White House switchboard."

Dr. Graves was conflicted. His patient did not seem to be concerned about this situation at all—did she know, remember more than she had let on? *Is the White House switchboard going to patch me through to talk to the President? Of course not*, the doctor thought.

"Thank you, Agent, I don't think that will be necessary. Ms. Coles is an adult. I can't keep her here if she chooses to leave against medical advice. I will have to note in her file that she is leaving against medical advice, and she'll need to sign for that."

Tommie finished dressing in the bathroom, freshened up, gathered the rest of her personal items, and looked around the room for anything she missed.

"I'm sorry to put you in this position, Dr. Graves. You've been wonderful. But I feel like I should go with the Agent. Would you like me to telephone you once I get settled over there? I'm happy to, to let you know I'm all right."

"Yes, I would appreciate that, Ms. Coles."

"Of course," Tommie said, then turned to the man in the suit. "Agent, I think I'm ready."

"Thank you, Ms. Coles, Doctor," Agent Smith nodded to the doctor. "Ms. Coles, we have a car waiting downstairs."

Tommie thanked Dr. Graves again, offered another apology, and followed Agent Smith out of the door and down the hallway she'd just begun taking walks down, past the nurse's station. There was a flurry of activity from a new, difficult patient admission, something the agents had counted on, and no one really noticed Tommie. Agent Smith had fallen back several steps, and had taken all of Tommie's personal items, even her purse. It looked like Tommie was just taking another hallway walk. The other agent had taken the stairwell near Tommie's room. They had gotten into the hospital and onto the ward without causing attention. No need to muck everything up getting out.

In the elevator, as hospital patients and personnel joined them, Tommie and Agent Smith pretended not to know each other, smiling politely, and nodding as other riders got on the elevator. At street level, Tommie immediately saw the black Suburban across the entrance in short-term parking. She walked toward the passenger-side backseat, opened the door, and slid in. Agent Smith closed the door behind her, walked around to the other side, and got in the backseat with her. The other agent was already in the driver's seat ready to pull out. Agent Smith leaned over and kissed Tommie on the cheek.

"You look good," he said, "for all you've been through."

"Thanks, LT, you too. Black site? Have you already debriefed?"

"Yes, I have. But we really *are* taking you to be cared for by White House doctors, President's orders. Not a rouse. He's been worried about you. Secretary Brown, too. Lots of people, for that matter."

"That's nice of him," Tommie said. But it wasn't *just* nice, she knew. She settled back into her seat and put her head on the headrest. She was tired. She wasn't well yet, not by a long shot. But it was nice to see Lawrence Tyler and feel safe again. She closed her eyes, leaning her head on Tyler's shoulder, and the driver hit the road.